AN ASIAN TRAGEDY

AN ASIAN
AMERICA AND VIETNAM
TRAGEDY

BY DAVID DETZER

The Millbrook Press
Brookfield, Connecticut

Map by Joe Le Monnier
Photographs courtesy of
James Pickerell, Black Star: pp. 15, 78; UPI/Bettmann:
pp. 20, 43, 70, 84, 111, 114, 131, 135, 139;
AP/Wide World Photos: pp. 32, 37, 40, 52, 92, 102, 121;
Bettmann Archive: p. 65; U.S. Army: p. 97 (both).

Library of Congress Cataloging-in-Publication Data

Detzer, David.
An Asian tragedy : America and Vietnam / by David Detzer.
p. cm.
Includes bibliographical references and index.
Summary: Examines the Vietnam War, from the early struggle
of the Vietnamese against foreign domination to American
intervention and the aftermath of the conflict.
ISBN 1-56294-066-X
1. Vietnamese Conflict, 1961–1975—United States—Juvenile
literature. 2. Vietnam—History—Juvenile literature.
[1. Vietnamese Conflict. 1961–1975.] I. Title.
DS558.D48 1992
959.704'3—dc20 91-37228 CIP AC

CONTENTS

To Melanie—
for all the reasons

THE LAND OF
HO CHI MINH

There is an ancient tale, a thousand years old, of a king
of England named Canute. Day after day he heard his
fawning courtiers tell him the same thing: "You are so
great, King Canute, you can do anything." He listened
in silence a long time, knowing the silliness of their
claims, but finally he grew impatient.

He ordered them to join him where the sea met the
land. He stood upon the sand, with them around him,
and shouted at the waters. "Don't rise," he demanded.
"Stop your tides," he told the sea.

The waters, of course, paid no attention. They lapped
quietly against the rocks, oblivious to the presence of
this great king. And the tide rose, as it had always done.

Canute smiled at his courtiers. He had made his
point. Not even a powerful king, with all his swagger
and all his armies, can do everything.

This tale has a simple moral: Some things are beyond the power of governments; some forces in the world
cannot be altered by armies.

The story of America and Vietnam is like this legend of Canute and the waters of the sea.

The history of Vietnam has resulted from the combination of three great forces: the land, the presence of the Chinese to the north, and the determination of the Vietnamese to be independent.

The story of every nation begins with the land and the climate. The first Vietnamese, whoever they were, lived in a region of Southeast Asia that has been called Tonkin. The central fact of this area is the Red River, which hurtles down from high mountain peaks not far away. As these waters, carrying their rich farm soil, reach the low-lying plains near the sea, they spread out like the fingers of a hand. Early farmers, seeing this land for the first time, must have smiled. Nature had provided all the major ingredients for agriculture—especially for rice farming. Here was flat land, easily tillable. Here was the warm sun (the delta lies along the same latitude as Key West, Florida), pleasant in the winter and relatively moderate in the summer. Not far away was the sea, which could supply the farmer with both salt and fish. (The three primary ingredients of the Vietnamese diet are still rice, salt, and fish.)

There is, however, one great flaw in this pleasant picture: When the rainy season begins, the Red River can move so rapidly, as it rushes out of the mountains, that it can become a maddened thing out of control, sweeping away everything in front of it. Farms and whole towns can disappear—unless the farmers control the river. Early settlers in the delta discovered that if they built dikes and dams and canals and gave the mighty river room to shoulder its way to the sea harmlessly, they could save their farms. But a dike or a dam is a huge project. A few individuals—a family, even a clan—cannot build it by themselves. Such an undertaking requires great effort by many people. Thus, the people of the Red River delta, of northern Vietnam, have had to learn to work hard and work together. Nature has offered them a fine bounty, but it has required that they develop a culture that has little use for any individual working alone, a culture that emphasizes the group.

For more than a thousand years the people of the delta spread around the great river and its tributaries. They built canals. They grew rice in paddies, hunching over in the sun, protected by their round, conical hats, to pull weeds and tend their plants. They ate the kernels of the rice plants and turned the rest into straw mats, into fertilizer, into wine and beer. They threw any excess to their pigs. Nothing went to waste. They discovered that the water buffalo, a great blue-gray beast, sometimes 6 feet (almost 2 meters) tall at the shoulder and weighing a ton, had incredible hooves that allowed it to move easily through the muck and the mud of the paddies. Photographs taken during the twentieth century have often shown little Vietnamese boys sitting atop some vast buffalo, moving it carefully through a paddy. These scenes are timeless; no doubt little boys and buffalo have been doing precisely the same things in those same fields for perhaps two thousand years.

Inland from the delta, as the flatlands rise into the mountains, the jungles begin. Today, half the country of Vietnam is still jungle. There, hidden in clearings, live the descendants of some of the aboriginal people of Vietnam. Racially they are slightly different from the rest of the population. They also do not farm as diligently as their lowland neighbors. They hunt for much of their food. They are less concerned with owning land than are the lowland Vietnamese; they tend to be more mobile and move across the land (like the nomadic

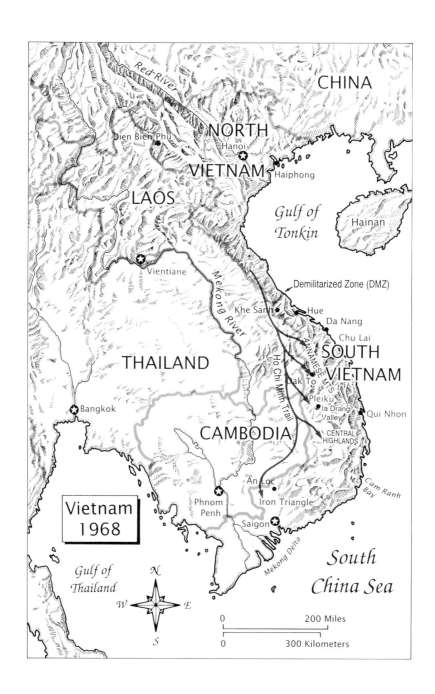

CHINA

Red River

NORTH
VIETNAM

Dien Bien Phu

Hanoi

Haiphong

Gulf of
Tonkin

Hainan

LAOS

Vientiane

Mekong River

Demilitarized Zone (DMZ)

Khe Sanh

Hue

Da Nang

Chu Lai

THAILAND

ANNAMESE MTS.

SOUTH
VIETNAM

Ho Chi Minh Trail

Dak To

Pleiku

Bangkok

Ia Drang
Valley

Qui Nhon

CAMBODIA

CENTRAL
HIGHLANDS

Vietnam
1968

An Loc

Iron Triangle

Cam Ranh
Bay

Phnom
Penh

Saigon

Gulf of
Thailand

N

Mekong Delta

South
China Sea

W   E

S

| 0 | 200 Miles |

| 0 | 300 Kilometers |

American Indians). The French, who came to this region in the 1800s, called them *montagnards* ("mountain people") because they lived in the hills. Most Vietnamese farmers, living down below on their neat farms, detested the montagnards and often referred to them as *mois* (generally translated as "savages"). (An infamous American once said, "The only good Indian is a dead Indian." That same attitude of racism and cultural contempt is similar to the feeling of most lowland Vietnamese toward the thirty-three tribes of montagnards.)

A Chinese army entered the delta in 111 B.C. and conquered it. Despite the Chinese domination, the Vietnamese retained their own language, an incredibly complex tonal language, in which the meaning of a word is almost completely dependent on the way it is pronounced. Each syllable can be spoken with one of six different vocal inflections, and each different tone has a different meaning. Their language, as a result, is terribly hard to learn and has created an almost impassable wall between most Vietnamese and outsiders, especially Westerners. During America's war in Vietnam, few Americans ever learned to speak to the people in their own language. The language barrier, probably more than anything else, made the Vietnamese seem "foreign" to Americans—and, no doubt, vice versa.

The first Vietnamese revolt against the Chinese came in A.D. 39. Others followed. In A.D. 938, after more than a thousand years of Chinese domination, the Vietnamese regained their independence. The Chinese later tried, off and on, to regain control of Tonkin, but except for one brief period in the fifteenth century they never succeeded. The Vietnamese, who had learned to work together to build their dikes and dams, also learned that national unity was necessary for defense. The heroes—and heroines—of their struggle against the Chinese are still remembered. Young Vietnamese are constantly reminded that their ancestors fought and died to gain or preserve their nation's freedom.

With the Chinese menace mostly behind them, the Vietnamese began a process familiar to Americans. The population grew, and people looked for new land to turn into rice paddies. Like those Americans who moved west from colonial Jamestown and Massachusetts Bay, the Vietnamese moved south along the coast. The mountains of Tonkin stretch southward, paralleling the coast. In one place they stand only 30 miles (48 kilometers) from the sea. Vietnamese farmers, preferring low-lying land, hugged the coastline.

South of Tonkin, in an area later called Annam, the Vietnamese butted into a kingdom called Champa, populated primarily by bloodthirsty pirates and merchants of various nationalities. The people, called Chams, began a war about A.D. 1000 when they attacked the Vietnamese. The conflict between the two peoples lasted until 1471, when finally the Vietnamese won.

Soon, even this land of Annam was not enough for the Vietnamese, and they expanded still farther southward. During the seventeenth century (about the time the first American settlers were pushing toward the Appalachians), the Vietnamese entered the vast, almost uninhabited expanse of another river delta, this one created by the Mekong River, which flowed 2,500 miles (4,000 kilometers) from mountains in Tibet. Because this river travels so much farther than the Red River of Tonkin, it is gentler and moves more slowly in the lowlands near the sea.

Here in this hot, humid Mekong Delta—at the same latitude as the country of Panama—the heavy rains and the great Mekong River create one of the best farming regions—especially one of the greatest rice-growing

*Vietnam's traditional farming methods
required hard work and cooperation. Here,
rice seedlings are loaded onto wagons.*

areas—of the world. The French called it Cochin China. The people of this area, with its plentiful land and its stifling heat and humidity, are more easygoing than the industrious northerners of the Red River delta.

The country of Vietnam has often been compared to one of those bamboo poles that Vietnamese peasants carry across their shoulders, supporting two large rice baskets, one on either end. The image is apt. In the north is the Red River delta—one rice basket. South, along the South China Sea, lies the slender "bamboo pole" of farmers and fishermen. Finally, in the far south is the Mekong Delta—the other rice basket.

The Vietnamese were still settling into their southern basket when the French arrived.

Europeans assumed that God was on their side, and they felt superior to heathens like the Vietnamese. The people of Europe were convinced they had the right to take over the non-European peoples of the world—it was their "Manifest Destiny," as Americans said. Europeans felt a patronizing contempt for all things that did not derive from the culture of Western Europe. And they felt it their obligation to provide Western culture to the unfortunate peoples of the world. The English poet Rudyard Kipling called it "the White Man's Burden." The French referred to it as their *mission civilisatrice* ("civilizing mission"). At the core of this "mission" was Christianity.

The first Christian missionaries arrived in Vietnam in the seventeenth century. They came from several European countries, but the most energetic and determined were from France. They came, they saw, and they converted. By the middle of the nineteenth century, tens of thousands of Vietnamese had converted to Catholicism. Some Vietnamese leaders resented this and sporadically persecuted Christians in Vietnam. These persecutions aroused many Frenchmen to anger and demands that their government do something. French merchants, meanwhile, were clamoring for increased trade in Asia.

Then, bubbling to the top of the French government came Louis Napoleon, an adventurer with a gambler's instinct. By luck and pluck he stumbled into the presidency of France. Since he was ambitious and was a distant relative of Napoleon Bonaparte, he decided in 1852 to declare himself Napoleon III, emperor of the French. Many Frenchmen at the time were willing to accept this charade, because Louis Napoleon promised a return to French *gloire*—the glory of the past. This sallow-faced, bearded, heavy-lidded man with a poet's soul and a Gallic nonchalance, however, needed to do something dramatic to prove his imperial worth. So he involved France in Italian politics and Mexican adventures. And, in 1858, he sent a French fleet to Vietnam.

The fleet arrived—with its excellent cannons—at the city of Saigon. Within a few years France controlled the southern part of Vietnam. During the next twenty years France expanded its power north along the coast, until in 1883 it had taken over all of Vietnam. Soon the French extended their control over neighboring Laos and Cambodia as well.

In Paris, the French examined maps of France's Asian holdings and dubbed them "Indochina" (meaning, the land between India and China). They put their administrative capital in the largest city in Tonkin: Hanoi. During the next few generations several thousand French citizens left France for Indochina. Their motives varied. Some went as administrators. Some went to spread the *mission civilisatrice*. Many went to make money. There was much money to be made.

The French used modern dredging equipment to build canals and drainage systems in Cochin China. The Mekong River delta soon became one of the world's greatest rice-growing areas. In the central highlands, 40 miles (65 kilometers) north of Saigon, the French brought in rubber plants and created vast rubber plantations. Companies like Michelin grew rich in the rubber business.

The French genuinely believed that they were doing wonderful things for Vietnam. They expanded and developed the city of Saigon; they built highways throughout the country to expand their businesses; they converted more than a million people to Catholicism; they brought in French law. Most of all, they carried French culture with them. French men and women living abroad, far from their mother country, felt disoriented without their customary trappings: French clothes, wines, music, food—and, of course, the French language. In 1910 a survey showed that only *three* of the French in all of Vietnam—out of all the priests, soldiers, businessmen, and administrators there—could speak Vietnamese with even moderate fluency. It was up to the Vietnamese, therefore, to learn French, a "civilized" language. Some Vietnamese were lucky enough, or shrewd enough, to do so; they had an excellent opportunity to make vast sums of money and acquire great power. They could easily rob their own people, since how would the French know?

Unfortunately, many French changes in Vietnam harmed the population. Traditionally, most Vietnamese believed that their nation's leaders should demonstrate three characteristics: education, virtue, and age. The French were less impressed with these qualities. Under French rule, Vietnamese who succeeded had to have other attributes, primarily wealth and connections.

The French government also specifically prohibited any industries in Vietnam that might compete with those of the mother country. Although Vietnam was one of the world's major rubber exporters, it manufactured almost no rubber products. For example, the Vietnamese had to import all their tires. And, although Vietnam was covered with forests, railroad companies imported railroad crossties from France.

Earlier, Vietnam had spent centuries fighting China to gain or maintain independence. Now, inevitably, the Vietnamese revolted against the French.

The first revolt erupted in 1885 and lasted for more than a decade; another started soon afterward. These complex struggles were wrapped in disease and starvation and guerrilla warfare—and failure.

Eventually, there came a man who called himself Ho Chi Minh.

The history of Ho Chi Minh's early life is sketchy. He was born in central Vietnam in 1890, the son of a wandering scholar. His name at that time was Nguyen Tat Thanh. Later on, he changed his name several times, generally to stay a step ahead of his enemies. He eventually adopted the name Ho Chi Minh; it means "he who enlightens."

When he was about sixteen, he entered a prestigious secondary school to prepare for a career in French colonial administration. He left, for some reason, without earning a diploma. His problems at the school were unlikely to have involved any intellectual shortcomings. Ho Chi Minh was extremely gifted, especially in languages. During his lifetime he became fluent in Vietnamese, French, English, Chinese, and Russian; he could also, when necessary, read or speak several other languages, including German.

After leaving the academy, apparently he took courses at a cooking school. Being a cook was not the sort of career that led to status in Vietnam, and no doubt his family was humiliated. But the training did lead to the next major step in his life. About 1911 or 1912, at

Ho Chi Minh, in a photograph taken in 1946.

the age of twenty-two, he became a cook on a French ship. During the next several years Ho traveled the globe. He apparently traveled to French Africa, to Europe, even to New York City.

Sometime during World War I (1914–1918), Ho went to Paris. By the time he arrived, the city had a fairly large enclave of Vietnamese immigrants, and he lived among them. He obviously read the proclamations of the American president, Woodrow Wilson, because Ho knew that Wilson declared that one of the results of this terrible war would be the freedom of "national peoples." Wilson was actually thinking only of Europeans, but Ho interpreted Wilson's words to mean people everywhere—including the Vietnamese.

In 1919, when Wilson arrived in Paris for peace discussions, Ho was ready. At this time he was referring to himself as "Nguyen the Patriot." He prepared a petition to present to Woodrow Wilson, requesting independence for his people. But the American president refused to even see him. Ho—or Nguyen the Patriot— appeared to Wilson's entourage just a slender, yellow-skinned twenty-nine-year-old colonial, not worthy of attention. Ho's hopes were dashed.

Meanwhile, Europe was in turmoil. Revolutionaries in Russia had recently toppled the czar's government. This single act, because of its stunning and unexpected success, caused oppressed peoples all over the world to feel an intense optimism for their own causes. If a small group of Russian radicals could succeed, perhaps the Russian Bolsheviks—the Communists—knew the secret of how to accomplish great changes.

In dozens of nations, where individuals felt that "the system" or "the establishment" was controlling them, people started to call themselves "Communists" and talked seriously of their own "revolutions." Ho Chi Minh was one of these.

Did he become a Communist because, of all political philosophies in the world at the time, Communism was the only one to oppose colonialism? Or did he become a Communist because he was drawn to Communism's radicalism, to its revolutionary goals? In other words, what was his primary motive? Was he a Vietnamese *nationalist* first, or was he primarily a Communist revolutionary? The answer is unclear, even today. Between 1920, when he first joined the French Communist party, and 1941, when he finally returned to Vietnam after being away from his homeland for thirty years, Ho Chi Minh was a full-time, active Communist functionary. He was a radical agitator and organizer, trained in the Kremlin, apparently willing to serve anywhere Moscow sent him. He popped up here and there in China, Russia, Thailand—and perhaps a dozen other nations. About 1937 or 1938 he was with China's Communist leader, Mao Zedong, hiding in China's northwest mountains. There he studied Mao's theories of guerrilla warfare. Later on, he would apply them in Vietnam, and American GIs would face the tactics Ho had learned from Mao.

Among Mao's writings is the story of an old man who began with his sons to dig up two vast mountains. All they had were simple hoes. Wrote Mao:

Another greybeard, known as the Wise Old Man, saw them and said derisively, "How silly of you to do this! It is quite impossible for you few to dig up these two huge mountains." But the other old man replied, "When I die, my sons will carry on; when they die, there will be my grandsons, and then their sons and grandsons, and so on to infinity. High as they are, the mountains cannot grow any higher and with every bit we dig, they will be that much lower. Why can't we clear them away?" [1]

Mao's moral in this tale was simple: Patience and determination can move—or eliminate—mountains.

Ho learned Mao's lessons well. The revolution Ho eventually initiated in Vietnam would continue after his death and succeed.

When Ho Chi Minh returned home in 1941, he was fifty-one years old, a pencil-thin little man with dark, sensitive, intelligent eyes and a wispy beard. He had a good sense of humor and was a fine writer and a good speaker. He was ascetic, virtually a monk. Apparently he never married.

Ho had returned to organize his people against a foreign power. But ironically it was not the French he came to fight; it was the Japanese.

During the 1930s, Japan fought a war with China. In its first few months the Japanese handily won all the battles. But surprisingly the Chinese government refused to concede and retreated into the mountains of southern China. There they received supplies from outside. Many of these supplies came through Vietnam by way of Haiphong, the major port in Tonkin. In 1940, desperate to cut off China's supply lines and realizing how weak France was because of losses it had recently sustained during the first months of World War II, the Japanese moved into Vietnam. They allowed local French officials to continue a fiction of control over the country, but Japanese soldiers ran things. It was this situation that brought in Ho Chi Minh.

Ho slipped across the border from southern China into Vietnam. He hid out in a jungle retreat and began to organize. He called his group the "Vietminh." They included radicals like himself, but they also included middle-class nationalists who had become convinced by the Japanese occupation that the French were weak and could be overthrown.

After the Japanese bombed Pearl Harbor in December 1941, the Americans looked on anyone fighting Japan as an ally. In Indochina only one group might be of service to America: the Vietminh. One day, American agents arrived at Ho Chi Minh's jungle headquarters. Out of this contact came an agreement: The United States would send aid to the Vietminh, and in return the Vietminh would spy on the Japanese and help American pilots shot down over Vietnam.

Ho Chi Minh believed that the American government supported his goal of independence for Vietnam. In a sense he was correct; President Franklin D. Roosevelt disliked the French Empire. But the fate of Vietnam was complicated by many outside factors.

By the time Japan was defeated in 1945, Roosevelt had died; Harry Truman had replaced him. One cannot know what Roosevelt would have done had he lived, but it was clear from the beginning that Truman felt himself under no obligation to an obscure Vietnamese named Ho Chi Minh. In the post–World War II years, Truman's major concern was a possible threat from the Soviet Union. To forestall that danger, he decided to give as much support as he could to France.

At the end of World War II, therefore, a tragedy was inevitable. France was determined to re-create its empire in Asia. And, like a girl dragging her reluctant beau to a dance, France would drag the United States into a war in Vietnam.

AMERICA AND THE COLD WAR

Wars seldom begin with simple clarity. Governments tend to stumble into wars, waffling back and forth between confidence and uncertainty. Later, when the smoke has settled and the bodies have been buried, historians examine the available facts, searching through the littered evidence like police at a crime scene, trying to account for what happened.

It is hard to know precisely when to begin the story of America's involvement in Vietnam, but one place to start might be Potsdam, Germany.

In July 1945, President Harry Truman, still new at the job, arrived in Potsdam to meet with other Allied leaders at the close of World War II. President Franklin D. Roosevelt had chosen him as a running mate in 1944. When Roosevelt had unexpectedly died in April 1945, Harry Truman was suddenly in the White House.

Truman was a trim man with thick glasses, burly around the chest. He drank whiskey, perhaps occasionally too much, and told dirty jokes. He was far from smooth. But he tended to have an engaging honesty about him and he did not normally shrink from hard decisions. It was a good thing. In Potsdam in 1945 he had to face the world's most powerful dictator, Joseph Stalin.

The Soviet Union was less than thirty years old. Stalin had ruled it for much of its history. He was short and stocky, his mustached face pitted, his eyes steady and absolutely pitiless. He had spent years killing his way to the top; once there, he had maintained power with a brutal police state. He killed, some reputable historians estimate, more than 20 million of his own people.

Yet at Potsdam Stalin was uneasy. Twice during his lifetime the Germans had attacked Russia. The two world wars had cost his people dearly. He thirsted for revenge. But more than that, he wanted to protect the Soviet Union from another attack by the Germans. He was determined to use the countries of Eastern Europe as a barrier against Germany.

While Truman was at Potsdam, he drove through the city of Berlin, a few miles away. The limousine moved slowly through the rubble of Hitler's capital, past the dazed German survivors. The city's people were still digging themselves out, looking for food or coal. A potato, eaten raw, was a day's wages in Berlin that summer. The combination of months of Allied bombing and the final maddened attack by the Soviet army had destroyed this center of Hitler's Third Reich. The stench inside the rubble still lingered in Berlin the day Truman drove through. The whole scene forced on him a powerful recognition of the dividends of World War II and of how much Europe had suffered in the war—and how weak it still was. During the next eight years President Truman focused much of his attention on rebuilding Western Europe. Part of his motive was humanitarian; the other part lay in his strong suspicion that unless

America helped Europe recover, Stalin's armies would move again, this time through Germany and all the way to the Atlantic.

Thus, throughout their various meetings at Potsdam, Truman and Stalin watched each other cautiously. The Cold War, the worldwide contest between the United States and the Soviet Union, had begun. America's war in Vietnam, on the other side of the globe, would be part of that struggle.

The Cold War started in ugliness, stinking of suspicion, of bullying. And it got worse.

Although Stalin was pathologically cautious, he gradually expanded Soviet power whenever he thought he could get away with it. He firmly believed that the United States wanted to destroy him, and he did everything he could to prepare himself for that coming conflict.

In a sense Stalin was not wrong to fear the United States. The American leadership did feel deep antagonism toward Stalin's regime and its philosophy of Communism. Americans began to view the whole world as a giant chess game between "our side"—increasingly referred to as the Free World—versus the Red Menace. Magazines and newsreels took to showing maps with an ominous stain spreading from the Soviet Union. The Red Menace, the maps suggested, was spreading like a virus across the globe. Politicians said it was America's duty to stem this tide. Anyone who opposed that viewpoint was considered weak or addled or, worst of all, to have a leaning toward Communism—such a person was labeled a "comsymp" (a Communist sympathizer), a leftist, a fellow traveler, a pinko.

Despite all the talk about the Red Menace, however, most Americans remained unsophisticated about the Soviet Union or Communism. To show their loathing for Communism, schools and even universities refused to offer courses on the subject. It was easier to remain smugly hostile.

Almost all Americans—including Truman and his successor in the White House, Dwight D. Eisenhower (and most of their advisers)—perceived Communism as a single unit, run like an efficient machine by Joseph Stalin and his henchmen in the Kremlin. This image of a "Communist monolith" directed by Moscow had a kernel of truth, but it was two-dimensional and therefore ultimately wrong.

To be sure, Stalin—and those who later took his place in the Kremlin—wanted to control, and even pretended to control, the actions of every Communist in the world. But they could not. Humans are not robots. They have many, and often contradictory, ambitions and feelings. A Communist normally believed devoutly in the goal of a "classless society" and the elimination of poverty. But that same Communist also had friends and family members to be concerned about, was part of a community, had a job, took vacations, listened to music, rooted for sports teams, worried about his or her health, and was frequently profoundly patriotic about his or her own nation. These people might go to Communist party meetings—in France, the United States, Poland, or Vietnam—where they would be told what the Kremlin's latest viewpoint was. But they absorbed or accepted only a certain percentage of what they were told. If the Moscow line contradicted one of their other basic loyalties—to their family, for example, or their nation—they would unconsciously, or even consciously, reject it. Fundamentally, most Communist Frenchmen were Frenchmen first. And that was true of Communists everywhere, including that isolated place called Vietnam.

America's leaders, however, usually refused to accept that fact.

In the fall of 1949 two events altered American history. In China the Communists, led by Mao Zedong, won what had been a long civil war. During the previous decade the American government had backed the other side. Now some of Truman's opponents blamed the American president for what was being called the "fall of China." How, they asked, did we "lose" China? The question itself was symptomatic of America's pride. It implied that China had been *ours* to lose. It had not been, of course.

The other critical event that autumn of 1949 was an explosion inside the Soviet Union. In early September, American intelligence informed Truman that the Russians had just detonated an atomic device. The Soviets had the Bomb. The United States and Great Britain no longer had a monopoly on this incredible weapon. Stalin, the greatest killer in the history of the world, had one too. The implications were frightening.

During the years after the Potsdam conference, American policy toward the Soviet Union had solidified. The United States, the White House decided, would "contain" the Russians. This policy of "containment" meant that the Americans would prevent the Soviets from expanding their power, to keep the Red Tide from staining more of the globe. The United States would ally itself with any country—or government—that seemed to be threatened by Moscow. Washington would provide it with money and arms. When this policy was first suggested, American leaders intended to apply it solely to Europe. It never dawned on them that they might have to worry much about Soviet power expanding elsewhere: Africa, the Caribbean, Southeast Asia.

When Americans thought of international affairs, they thought of Europe. In 1945 most of the world was still divided up among the so-called Great Powers, those countries that had world empires. These included, especially, Great Britain and France. The United States had drawn much of its culture from these two nations. America might not always agree with them, but it respected them.

In the 1950s, American high school students read world history textbooks that devoted perhaps a single chapter to Asia and had only passing references to Africa, the Middle East, and Latin America. Even high school courses on Europe were narrow. Students virtually never learned the complexities of Eastern Europe, or even Scandinavia or Spain. Mainly they studied Britain, France, and Germany. Everything else out there was distant and foggy and seemed of little importance—until China "fell" to Communism.

Given the theory of the Communist monolith, the success of Mao implied the expansion of Stalin's power. Many Americans now thought that the Soviets had *control* over China, the most populous country in the world. Could the rest of Asia be far behind? American intelligence knew that there were local Communist parties in half a dozen Asian nations. The British were fighting a Communist rebellion in Malaya. The Philippine government was attempting to suppress Communist insurgents called Huks. And in Vietnam there was Ho Chi Minh.

Under the sudden one-two impact of the discovery of Soviet atomic power and Mao's success in China, Truman made a decision. He ordered his government to consider the implications of these two events, to rethink what needed to be done. His orders went out—to the State Department, to the military, and so on, filtering deep within the bowels of the American government.

Throughout the winter of 1949–50, his administration examined the problem. Specialists in each section pondered, discussed, analyzed. Then they drew up their proposals and handed them to their bosses. Their bosses combined the suggestions and handed their conclusions to *their* bosses. Up through the bureaucracy percolated the ideas.

In April 1950 the highest advisers to the president, the National Security Council (NSC), met. They reviewed everything and came up with their final suggestions. Their proposal, which was highly secret, came to be known simply by its bureaucratic number, NSC-68. Truman read it and initialed it, indicating that he approved of its contents.

NSC-68 is one of the most important documents in American history, yet it *still* remains secret. Historians, however, have pieced together its basic outlines. The document proposed that the United States drastically increase its own military power, that it also arm its European allies, that it take a hard stand against Communism in Asia, including China, the Philippines, and Vietnam. All of this would cost a great deal of money and would take determination. The essence of the document was simple: The Communist threat had become worldwide, and the United States must act as a global policeman.

A few weeks later came the first test. A large North Korean military force, armed by the Soviet Union, crashed across the border with South Korea. Would the United States enter this conflict—which was, in many senses, a civil war between two parts of the same nation? Truman pondered his options for a few days and then made his decision. He sent American soldiers into Korea. For the next two months the issue was in doubt, but eventually the United States began to win. The North Koreans were pushed back. The Americans followed. They considered crossing the border that separated the

*A gun crew prepares to fire on North Korean
positions from the center of Seoul, the
capital of South Korea. The bitter conflict
devastated large sections of the country.*

two governments, North and South Korea. Here, in this part of Asia, the policy of "containment" seemed outdated. Why not push the Communists out of a country—North Korea—they already controlled?

From Mao in Peking came a signal to the United States: If the American military did actually shoulder its way into North Korea, China would enter the war. Washington thought the Chinese were bluffing. In October 1950, American troops hurtled into North Korea. On Thanksgiving Day their grateful government flew traditional Thanksgiving meals to its soldiers near the northern border of North Korea. The GIs chowed down on turkey with cranberry dressing, buttered squash, mince pie, and the rest of the trimmings. Each soldier was even provided his own after-dinner mint. Their generals declared that the troops would be home by Christmas, or soon thereafter.

The next day 300,000 Chinese soldiers, who had spent the past eight weeks slipping around the Americans and hiding in the hills, attacked. It was a stunning military surprise. The Americans retreated—and retreated. They went back hundreds of miles, the longest military retreat in American history.

Eventually, the American lines solidified again and the Chinese were stopped. The two sides took up positions along the old border between North and South Korea, and they beat each other bloody for more than two years. It showed the White House and the Pentagon, and anyone else who cared to notice, that the Chinese Army was a serious foe and that Mao was determined to keep the United States far away from China's borders. The war in Korea straggled to a bitter end during the midsummer of 1953.

Less than a year later, while the Korean wounds were still fresh and painful in Washington, the United States became deeply involved in Vietnam.

3

THE ELEPHANT AND THE TIGER

There is an ancient Vietnamese tale about a fight to the death between an elephant and a tiger. The elephant was bigger and more powerful, of course, but the tiger was more ruthless and cunning. Instead of fighting on the ground where the elephant's vast strength made it invulnerable, the tiger leapt upon the elephant's back and bit it deep. The elephant, in its agony, screamed and reared. The tiger simply sprang to one side. Then, when the elephant wasn't looking, the tiger again jumped on the elephant's back and bit it deeper still. The blood flowed down the elephant's side. Gradually, the great gray pachyderm, the more powerful beast, weakened. And finally it died.

The tiger—clearly a smaller animal—had triumphed.

In the same way the Vietnamese would defeat two great Western powers, two elephants: first France, then the United States.

World War II was hardly over, the guns had hardly cooled, when a new war broke out in Vietnam, this time between the Vietminh and France.

In August 1945, Japan admitted defeat, and World War II was over. Japanese troops stationed in Vietnam surrendered to the Vietminh. Within days, Ho Chi Minh's organization took over the entire country. Remarkably, after five years of Japanese occupation, there was virtually no disorder or violence.

A few weeks later Ho addressed a huge crowd in a public square in Hanoi. "We hold that all men are created equal," he said, "that they are endowed by their Creator with certain unalienable Rights, among them are Life, Liberty and the pursuit of Happiness." Any American who might have heard or read his speech would have recognized the words, but Ho was perfectly willing to admit their source. "This immortal statement," he said, "is extracted from the Declaration of Independence of the United States of America in 1776." [2]

The crowd in the Hanoi plaza cheered and cheered. For the first time in almost a century Vietnam was again free. Circumstances and the little man with a wispy beard had given them independence. The bad days of colonialism seemed to be behind them.

It was, however, not going to be that simple.

France was determined to regain all the pieces of its empire that it had lost during World War II—including Vietnam. At first the United States was not especially sympathetic. But Truman felt that a stable and happy France was important for *European* stability, whereas the desires of an obscure people like the Vietnamese did not seem as important. So the United States backed France's return to power in Indochina. Ho Chi Minh and the Vietminh were ordered to turn over control of Vietnam to the French.

Ho Chi Minh hesitated imperceptibly but then agreed. He hoped something could be worked out with the French, some long-term agreement that would give Vietnam eventual independence. For a year between 1945 and 1946 he tried. The French rebuffed all his efforts. The result was inevitable: War broke out between France and the Vietminh.

This time Ho Chi Minh and his organization were all alone. The United States had abandoned them; the Soviet Union was far away and uninterested in this distant colonial struggle; Mao Zedong was having his own troubles at the time in China, simply staying alive in his Chinese civil war.

The Vietminh had to fight with whatever weapons were available. They had a few rifles and small arms, taken from the Japanese or given them by the Americans. But much of what they used in this war with the French were the classic weapons of guerrillas. The French had trucks and planes and artillery. The Vietminh had homemade bombs and punji stakes.

A punji stake was as good a symbol of this war— the French began to call it the "dirty war"—as anything. It was made of a metal nail or, more often, a bamboo stick sharpened to a deadly point. The Vietminh dug a hole in some well-beaten path where French soldiers might walk. Into the base of the hole, a foot or so beneath the surface of the ground, were hammered several of these stakes. The person who secretly placed them there often covered their points with a type of poison made of human excrement. The poison was not usu-

Soldiers move past a ditch filled with punji sticks. The sharp spikes were used by Vietnamese guerrillas against French and, later, American troops.

ally fatal, but if it cut the skin, it could cause a very nasty infection. The punji trap was then concealed with large leaves.

An unsuspecting French soldier could step in this hole. The sharp point of the stake might go through the sole of his boot or, failing that, would glance upward, as the soldier stumbled awkwardly, and ram itself into the soft muscles of the soldier's calf. It was painful, of course. But it was more than that. The soldier would have to be evacuated to a hospital to have his wound cared for. Someone, often two or three other soldiers, would have to carry him and his equipment. Thus a simple stick or nail could disable, and remove from the area, several well-armed professional French soldiers.

A punji stake, moreover, could be made and placed in its sinister hiding place by unexpected members of the Vietnamese population: an elderly woman, a young teenage girl, a little boy. (It might be noted that the Vietnamese would use precisely these same sorts of devices against the Americans twenty years later—and with great success. Someone once estimated that perhaps forty percent of America's casualties in its war in Vietnam came from punji stakes and similar hidden weapons.)

Punji stakes had many advantages to a guerrilla force like the Vietminh. They made the French insecure. Each Frenchman in Vietnam had to wonder, who was the enemy? Was it that small child sitting atop a water buffalo in the field? Was it that old crone, her skinny shoulders bent over her hoe in the rice paddy? Was it that sweet-faced girl walking by, her eyes modestly downcast and half-hidden by her conical thatched hat? Who could know? All Vietnamese seemed to look the same to the outsiders. If you didn't speak the language, you couldn't ask them. And, even if you did, could you believe what they said? Everyone heard stories about how this taxi driver or that secretary, this houseboy or that trusted translator turned out to be a secret, and dangerous, member of the Vietminh.

The French became maddened by the determined, continued, merciless opposition of this hidden enemy who seemed everywhere and nowhere. The French tried persuasion. They also tried torture. They took suspected groups of Vietminh up in planes and threw them off one by one, trying to frighten those still alive into revealing their plans. Nothing worked. The French had been trained to fight in a certain way—to charge like Napoleon's soldiers, or the valiant knights at Agincourt, or the troops in the thousand other battles the French had fought during fifteen hundred years. If only the Vietnamese would come out and fight like men—like Frenchmen.

Bit by bit the Vietminh squeezed the outsiders. They set up ambushes along isolated highways, and French soldiers increasingly refused to travel in small groups outside the towns. The nights belonged to the Vietnamese. The French virtually never dared move after dark. The rustling they heard in the underbrush might be an animal, or it might be a Vietminh killer.

Matters became worse after 1949. Mao won in China, and he was more than willing to help Ho Chi Minh fight the Europeans along China's southern border. Better weapons slipped across the line between China and northern Vietnam.

General Vo Nguyen Giap, who headed Ho Chi Minh's military force and had helped Ho create the Vietminh in 1941, was once asked the secret of successful warfare. He declared that the really important factor was always the same: "Human beings! Human beings are the decisive factor."[3] What he meant was that a soldier's spirit, his will, was more significant than his weapon. Weapons, of course, were important, Giap noted, but if a soldier feels a strong sense of mission—say, patriotism—he is willing to endure the inevitable

*General Vo Nguyen Giap, leader of the Vietminh
forces, with Ho Chi Minh in 1945.*

hardships of war. It is this endurance, this determination to continue against all odds, that was the secret to the ultimate success of the Vietminh.

Late in 1953 the French decided to trick Ho Chi Minh. They began to fortify an isolated spot called Dien Bien Phu in the western corner of Tonkin, not far from the border of Laos. They hoped to lure Giap into attacking this tempting morsel. Since they had failed to force the Vietminh into a "normal" battle, the French generals believed they could entice Ho and Giap into attacking *them*. Then, if that worked, the French would smash them. The French had an airfield at Dien Bien Phu to receive supplies and reinforcements if necessary. It seemed a cunning plan.

In a way it worked: Early in 1954 the Vietminh did prepare to attack the French garrison at Dien Bien Phu. Unfortunately for the French, their generals had made a serious miscalculation. Dien Bien Phu was near the middle of a small valley, completely surrounded by hills. The French had assumed that Giap's soldiers would be able to attack Dien Bien Phu only with small arms, rifles and some machine guns. What the French overlooked was the possibility that Giap could bring heavy artillery into the hills. This oversight was understandable. It seemed impossible that anyone, especially a backward guerrilla army, could maneuver heavy machinery like artillery through the trackless jungles around the valley and then push them somehow over the crests of the mountains. Each artillery shell was more than a single man could carry, and a siege of Dien Bien Phu would require tens of thousands of such shells.

But Giap, a military magician, made a modern army appear. By the time the actual battle began, Giap had almost 50,000 soldiers in position around the French, and he had placed heavy artillery in the hills, too. Another 31,500 peasant-porters had carried the guns, often piece by piece, through jungle paths the 500 miles (800 kilometers) from the Chinese border. These big guns could harass the 13,500 French troops by day and by night. More important, the artillery was able to destroy the airfield soon after the fighting began. Now the French were themselves isolated and trapped, with weapons that were inferior to those of their enemies. They were caught in precisely the trap they had prepared for the Vietminh.

The French soldiers fought valiantly and long. The battle began in March and lasted until May. French losses, including those captured, were enormous. It was a terrible blow.

The "dirty war" had lasted for eight years, from 1946 to 1954. In France the voters had grown disgusted with it. Too many French soldiers had died or been wounded, too much money had been spent, too much French pride had been lost. Tales of atrocities committed by French soldiers sickened reasonable French citizens; stories of murder and torture, filtering back to France, hardly seemed part of a *mission civilisatrice*. French politicians, feeling the Gallic pulse, increasingly announced their opposition to this war. By 1954, even before the Dien Bien Phu debacle, French leaders, reflecting public sentiment, were demanding an end to all this. They agreed to hold discussions with their enemy in Geneva, Switzerland.

The Korean War had ceased only a few months earlier. The United States remained extremely hostile toward Mao's China and the Soviet Union. Any Communist success, anywhere in the world, was viewed as a defeat for America.

The United States had been aiding France's war in Vietnam since 1950; by 1954 it was providing eighty

French soldiers defend the air base at Dien Bien Phu from trenches during a siege that lasted from March to May 1954.

percent of the financing of the "dirty war." During the last days of the battle of Dien Bien Phu, the United States nearly intervened directly to stop the Vietminh. The French government pleaded with Eisenhower, who had become president in 1953, to send *direct* military aid: the American navy, its air force, perhaps even its soldiers. Several of Eisenhower's top advisers were in favor of it. The president himself was uncertain, but he leaned toward military intervention. In fact, he ordered an American fleet to sail toward the Tonkin Gulf; it carried two hundred planes that could bomb, and perhaps destroy, Giap's artillery. The fleet secretly carried an additional weapon, the atomic bomb. If regular bombing failed, some of Eisenhower's advisers wanted the United States to use its nuclear might on the hills around Dien Bien Phu.

About this time Eisenhower was asked why his government cared what happened in such a far-off backwater of the world. He firmly stated that Vietnam was in fact an important, even a crucial, region. He noted that Southeast Asia provided the world with tin, tungsten, and rubber. He added that if Vietnam fell to Communism, the other nations in the area would fall to the same force. "The loss of Indochina," he said, "will cause the fall of Southeast Asia like a set of dominoes." [4]

Thus the "domino theory" was born. If one country in a region became Communist, the Red Virus could spread to all its neighbors. If Vietnam fell to Ho Chi Minh, the theory assumed, then Cambodia and Laos would inevitably become Communist—and then Thailand, Malaysia, Indonesia, and the Philippines. Who knew where the disease might stop?

Yet, when the battle of Dien Bien Phu caused the French government to ask Eisenhower for help, Eisenhower decided to consult several of Congress's top leaders. He had no intention of falling into the trap that Truman had, when the latter took the United States into Korea without consulting Congress. Eisenhower invited eight congressional leaders to the White House, had the situation explained to them, and asked for their reaction. They replied that the United States should *not* become involved in Vietnam unless U.S. action was part of a multinational effort—that is, the United States alone should not act like some sort of international police. As a result of this meeting, Eisenhower concluded that he would do nothing about Dien Bien Phu until he had first talked to the British. As it turned out, the British government was opposed to getting involved. So Eisenhower backed off.

The question of Vietnam would be decided, instead, in Geneva, Switzerland.

The meeting in Geneva involved the leaders of most of the world's greatest powers—France, Great Britain, the United States, China, the Soviet Union—and various factions and nationalities from Indochina. Each group had its own agenda. The French hoped for some sort of compromise that would allow them to retain a kernel of power in Indochina. The United States was determined to maintain its opposition to *any* compromise with "Communism" in Southeast Asia: therefore it would accept *no* agreement with Ho Chi Minh. (Washington was more intransigent about the Vietminh than France; that fact was an ominous portent for the future.)

Luckily, both major Communist regimes in the world, China and the Soviet Union, were anxious for some sort of settlement in Indochina. The Kremlin, still emerging slowly from the Stalin era, wanted time, and peace, to settle its internal matters. Mao's China was participating in its first real international conference. It wanted to seem a reasonable member of the world community. In addition, it was not anxious to have the United States fighting Ho Chi Minh along its southern border. In light of the Korean War, recently over, the Chinese considered it prudent to keep the United States far away.

Almost all Vietnamese factions were opposed to any compromises. They were adamantly against any division of their nation. But as the days of the conference went by, the Chinese and Soviet delegations put considerable pressure on the Vietminh to come to some agreement. At last the Vietminh relented.

The final agreements were called the Geneva Accords. They provided that Indochina would be divided into three independent countries, and only three: Laos, Cambodia, and Vietnam. Temporarily, for the next two years, Vietnam would be split into two sections along the 17th parallel, approximately in the middle. Ho Chi Minh would control the northern half; a non-Communist government would supervise the southern half. To try to ensure that incidents between the two sections would not occur, neither side would be permitted to place soldiers or military hardware within a bank of land a few miles wide that divided them, a "demilitarized zone" (DMZ).

Since many of Giap's Vietminh soldiers lived south of the DMZ, the agreement further provided that anyone who wished to do so could move north. As it turned out, when Ho Chi Minh ordered many southern members of his Vietminh to leave their homes and families and move north, many of them were distinctly unhappy. Their only compensation, they felt, was that this move was temporary. They had precisely three hundred days to "regroup," almost a year, but they expected to return soon.

The Geneva agreement clearly stated that in two years the people of Vietnam must hold an open election throughout the *entire* country, north and south of the DMZ. The regroupees (as those who moved north were called) felt confident that Ho Chi Minh would inevitably win. How could he lose? He was by far the most famous and popular person in Vietnam. The war against France had been fought largely in his name. He was the George Washington of Vietnam. No one could doubt that he was a shoo-in in the coming election. The regroupees would be able to return home as soon as the election took place in 1956. They would only be away from home, therefore, a little more than a year.

Ho Chi Minh himself did not like the Geneva compromise, but the pressure from China and the Soviet Union forced him to accept it. He, like the regroupees, looked to the coming election to settle this matter.

Ho Chi Minh's delegates never considered the possibility of *two* Vietnams. Vietnam was a single nation, with one language and one culture. It ought to have a single government. Any political division could only be temporary. The Vietminh delegation accepted the Geneva Accords only because of the provision for a 1956 election. It seemed frustrating to divide their country into halves; but if it took that to get the French out, then they would grudgingly agree.

A historian once noted that the American Revolution was really about two overlapping issues. It had certainly been about "home rule"—that is, whether the British would continue ruling their American colonies. But it had also been about "who should rule at home." In other words, once the British were ousted, who, or which faction, should take their place? During the early history of the United States, after the British were defeated, Ameri-

[47]

cans faced many arguments, fights, and revolts over what the future of America would be.

Experience suggested that what had happened in America in the eighteenth century would now inevitably occur in Vietnam. The French—like the British in America two centuries earlier—had been ousted. Now came the question: Who was going to rule in Vietnam?

At the end of the Geneva meeting there were two ominous developments. The United States refused to sign the accords. So did the "State of Vietnam," the political agency that was given control over southern Vietnam until the elections. A new prime minister had recently been selected in the South. His name was Ngo Dinh Diem. He firmly opposed the Geneva agreements.

AMERICA'S MANDARIN
FRIEND, DIEM

During the thousand years China controlled Vietnam, it took much from the Vietnamese people, but it gave some things in return. One was the Confucian tradition of the "mandarins."

Confucianism, which evolved during the sixth century B.C. and was named for the philosopher Confucius, proposed that each person held a place inside a series of concentric rings to which he or she owed loyalty. The first ring was the family. Then came the village, then the national government, then the cosmos. Each individual had to accept willingly his or her own place in the order of the world. One should love and trust one's family—including one's ancestors and one's descendants. One should also dutifully accept the state, because it was an extension of the family.

The leader of a government, like a good father, provided protection and was a good role model. Subjects, like children, were duty-bound to love and obey. Each government held its place because Heaven willed it so. One must be obedient to any government that fostered stability and prosperity because stability and prosperity showed that the government had the Mandate of Heaven. On the other hand, if the government allowed disorder, if the economy went sour, if even the weather became disrupted, then clearly the government had lost the Mandate of Heaven. And one need not owe it loyalty any more.

In the Chinese tradition, it was the duty of certain individuals to serve the government. They were called mandarins. They were supposed to be wise and cultured. They indicated these traits in a very simple way: They took an exam. The better one did on the test, the higher the position one could hold.

Imagine that the United States chose its officials this way. Those interested in government service would take a national exam. Judges would have to achieve certain scores, governors other scores, and so on. The president, presumably, would have to get the highest grade.

These exams required that one be literate and cultured. They tested would-be mandarins on Chinese literature, philosophy, poetry, and history. The system assumed that a man of "literate culture" was a person of the highest worth. If a mandarin needed things done that required particular skills, he could simply hire specialists—engineers or architects or military experts. The highest quality—wisdom, which came from the study of culture—could not be hired.

Under Chinese domination, Vietnam acquired the Confucian practice of the mandarinate. Even after Vietnam ousted China, it kept this tradition. During two millennia Confucianism sent down deep but subtle roots within the Vietnamese population. The average peasant held unusually strong emotional ties to his family—much more than most peasant societies outside Asia. When the French took over Indochina, they discouraged Confucianism. The last mandarin exams in Vietnam were given around 1900. But the concept remained.

It has sometimes been suggested that Ngo Dinh Diem was the last of the Vietnamese mandarins.

Diem looked distinctly like a penguin. He had jet black, heavily greased hair that he parted on the side and brushed down severely around his round head. He was short and plump, with very wide hips. He walked in an odd, awkward, open-toed way. Yet his appearance was deceiving. In fact, Diem was an immensely proud, austere man. His strengths and weaknesses came from the same source: He devoted himself completely to his nation. But he believed he was vastly apart from—and better than—his people. He apparently neither liked them nor understood them. He did not feel it necessary to win his people's support. He considered it their duty to love and obey him. He gave an impression of great self-control and distant coolness. That was the mandarin way.

Diem's good qualities included his personal honesty and his capacity for hard work. Many members of his government stole vast sums of money—not Diem. As a young man, he had seriously considered entering the Catholic priesthood and had spent much time in a Catholic seminary. He never lost a certain quality of asceticism. He worked sixteen or eighteen hours each day.

Ngo Dinh Diem was born in 1901. His father had made a great deal of money dealing with the French and had made sure his children were good Catholics. When Diem was young, he planned to enter France's colonial administration. He went to a school for would-be administrators and then climbed rapidly within the colonial bureaucracy, which the French allowed Vietnamese to

*Ngo Dinh Diem (standing, second from left)
with members of his family in 1963. Several,
including his brother Nhu (on Diem's right),
held high positions in government.*

enter. Eventually, however, he grew uncomfortable. It dawned on him that France's supercilious attitude toward the Vietnamese, its obvious feeling of superiority, meant that no Vietnamese could ever hope for real power in Vietnam. It was not in his nature to join nationalistic bomb throwers, so he merely withdrew into reclusiveness. Diem was a contemplative man by nature. If he had entered the priesthood at this time of his life, he probably would have been a very good scholar-priest.

After the Geneva Accords, the American government supported him because it appreciated what it considered his good qualities. It recognized that he was well trained in government work and it liked that in him. It also knew he had long been a good Vietnamese nationalist, that he had not allowed himself to get too close to the French. Diem's anti-French attitudes made him more attractive to the Americans. Even though France had signed the Geneva Accords, it clearly hoped to remain a kind of father figure to the Indochinese. Eisenhower's administration had other plans. From the vantage point of Washington, the French had failed in Southeast Asia and should go away and let the United States handle things. By backing Diem, Washington was opposing *both* Communism and French colonialism. It seemed a fine moral stance.

In northern Vietnam, Ho Chi Minh was not having an easy time. During the eight years before 1954, most of the fighting between the Vietminh and the French had taken place in Tonkin. As a result, that region had suffered the most serious damage. Its economy was shattered, and its infrastructure—including almost all its major highways and railroads—was devastated. In addition, when the French pulled out of Tonkin after the Geneva Accords, they purposely sabotaged much of the region in a disgruntled act of pure meanness. Partly as a result, food supplies in the North were low after 1954, and only aid from the Soviet Union and China helped Ho Chi Minh avert serious famine.

Ho's government in Hanoi was based on the Soviet model, a dictatorship percolating its power all the way down to the village level. This resulted in a variety of difficulties, but perhaps the primary problems involved food—and land ownership. In a rural, peasant society such as Vietnam's, control of agricultural land is vital. Large landowners dominate society and control most of the wealth; others depend on them for their living.

Ho "socialized" the agricultural land, intending, like Robin Hood, to take land from the rich and distribute it among the poor. Unfortunately for his plan, northern Vietnam did not have enough "rich" landholders. Many mid-level peasants therefore had their farmland confiscated. Those who objected were imprisoned; many were executed.

The brutality and the murders continued in the North for several years. Ho Chi Minh even faced the discomforting fact of some actual rebellions. Eventually, Ho called a halt to his agrarian "reforms." He released the prisoners, and he publicly apologized for the abuses.

Such events hardly formed a pretty picture, but in Ho's defense it might be noted that "bad times" seem to be an unfortunate but normal offspring of civil or revolutionary wars. In that sense Ho Chi Minh's problems were not surprising.

Neither were Ngo Dinh Diem's. One of Diem's first problems, however, was unexpected. When the Geneva agreements had allowed three hundred days for anyone who wished to do so to move across the DMZ, the assumption had been that most of those who would take advantage of this opportunity would be members of the

Vietminh who lived in the South and might prefer to settle in Ho's North. No one expected that a huge group of *northerners* might use this clause in the Geneva Accords to move southward, but that is what happened.

As soon as the agreement was signed, Catholic leaders in Tonkin began to lead their flocks south, away from the "atheistical Communists" of Ho Chi Minh. This migration was massive. Perhaps a million people, mostly poor peasants, poured into Diem's southern Vietnam—and became his responsibility. He already had more than enough trouble. Diem's first task was to provide some sort of political and social stability to his section—"South Vietnam," as it was being called in America's newspapers. Whenever a colony achieves independence, there is a sorting-out period, as various factions vie with each other. In South Vietnam this period was complicated by the human tidal wave of immigrants from the North.

During his first two years in power, Diem worked diligently to solve the problems, or at least deal with them. Surprisingly, he had remarkable success. He persuaded some of his opponents to join him; others he bought off. Still others he crushed with police or military ruthlessness. To be sure, he had significant financial support from the United States, but that by itself could not have accounted for all his successes. Diem really did possess many of the personal qualities necessary for such a complex situation. He had intelligence, determination, and subtle toughness.

Diem faced, however, one dilemma that seemed to have no easy solution. In July 1956, Vietnam was supposed to hold an election throughout both North and South—to determine which government would rule the entire nation. Without question, despite Diem's success in achieving a certain amount of stability in the South, an open Vietnamese election would go to Ho Chi Minh. The old radical, Uncle Ho, was still the only national hero to most Vietnamese. Diem could hardly have competed with an icon.

So, when the election came due, he ignored it. He just refused to hold it in the South. He felt under no obligation to do so since he had refused to sign the Geneva Accords. The United States backed Diem in his decision to ignore the election. In Hanoi, Ho Chi Minh was enraged, but there was nothing he could do—at first.

Historians and military analysts still disagree about many aspects of the Vietnam War. One debatable question involves the origins of the revolt that began late in the 1950s against Diem. Was this revolt triggered by orders from Hanoi? Or did southerners initiate it on their own?

This question is important because its answer defines what sort of conflict the Vietnam War was. American officials at that time saw the struggle as a war between two ''countries'': ''North Vietnam'' and ''South Vietnam.'' To others, this image was absurd. ''Vietnam'' was not two countries—it was a single nation. Therefore the struggle was a civil war. The riddle of who started the revolt against Diem made the matter even more murky. If Ho Chi Minh did not order it, then the war began entirely in the South, and it was unquestionably a civil war, even a social conflict.

If the United States was merely supporting one side—South Vietnam—in a conflict between two ''countries,'' Americans could feel that they were protecting the South against the North, and their actions fell within an understandable and acceptable role. Americans could view themselves as ''good guys''—something they much preferred to do, even needed to do. They could feel especially moral if the two countries represented the Communist Menace on the one hand and the Free World on the other. But if America was supporting a single faction in a complex internal social struggle within South Vietnam, then it would be difficult to see the United States' role in such a neat black-and-white way.

Since about 1985, Vietnamese officials have stepped forward and made statements concerning this riddle, but unfortunately their responses have often contradicted each other. A prominent American expert on the war, Stanley Karnow, stated in 1990 in *The New York Times* that North Vietnam actually began this revolt. Other historians have disagreed. So the answer about the war's beginnings, like much else about this conflict, still lies hidden in a fog of confusion and uncertainty.

One thing is clear: Simple orders from Hanoi by themselves would not have been enough to explain the revolt. Those who first rose against Diem—the cadres—were people of profound courage who were not robots.

Before 1954 a "cadre" was someone who held an important role within the Vietminh organization. Cadres organized and led their organization at the local level. They might be political cadres or military cadres. They were not necessarily major leaders; often they were local peasants. But they had been trained to organize others. The word *cadre* itself is French and means a "framework" (around which others gather). One would not consider Ho Chi Minh or Giap cadres. A cadre was equivalent to, say, a sergeant in the U.S. Army or a political organizer inside a Republican precinct in Des Moines, Iowa. A cadre's expertise and devotion were important. No organization can be successful without hardworking "sergeants" and "precinct captains."

Some cadres were Communists, some were not. No one can be sure how many were one or the other. Before 1954, most cadres had clearly wanted to throw France out of Indochina *and* had wanted to achieve some major social changes in Vietnam, including redistribution of the land. These attitudes hardly made them Communists, but after 1954 those goals would have put them in opposition to conservatives like Diem who were opposed to any sort of social and economic change.

By the time of Dien Bien Phu and the downfall of France, the Vietminh controlled much of southern Vietnam, as well as the North. Although many cadres "regrouped" to the North after 1954, at least three thousand remained in the South. These so-called "stay-behinds" continued to organize and train young recruits to the Vietminh. Diem knew about them and did not trust them. He successfully crushed many of their local training units, or cells. And because he knew that the name "Vietminh" held strong positive connotations for most Vietnamese, who remembered that it had been the Vietminh who had overthrown France, Diem took to calling the cadre organization in the South the "Vietcong" (that is, the "Vietnamese Communists"). It was Diem, therefore, who created that famous label.

(Later on, the American military, who had a tendency to use acronyms, called these Vietcong the "VC." Furthermore, American soldiers were trained, when using static-distorting radios, not to use mere letters when transmitting information; a "V" or a "C" might be confused with another similar letter, a "B" or a "Z." To avoid such mistakes, soldiers were told to refer to letters of the alphabet by obvious code words. The letter "A" became Alpha, "B" became Baker, and so on. The VC were therefore called "Victor Charlie." By early in the war American GIs had even taken to calling their enemy, whom they had come to respect, simply "Charlie.")

The revolt of the cadres in South Vietnam began in 1957. They had waited impatiently for the inevitable success of Ho Chi Minh in the 1956 elections; but when Diem refused to hold an election, the cadres acted.

First, they began to rebuild their organization, which had almost been destroyed by Diem's attacks on it. They rid themselves of some of their weaker cohorts and recruited new ones. Some of the regroupees, homesick and discouraged after Diem bypassed the election, trickled back to the South and joined them. Then, in late 1958, a representative from Ho went to South Vietnam to see for himself what was going on there. He returned to Hanoi and reported that the southern cadres were about to initiate an uprising, whether or not the North joined them. In May 1959 a meeting of Communists in Hanoi called for a North Vietnamese base to aid the South Vietnamese in their efforts to overthrow Diem, and to expel the United States. In a sense that decision was a major step down the road to the next phase of this almost endless war.

The size and efficiency of the Vietcong expanded rapidly. Hanoi provided guidance, to be sure. This was done through an organization called the Central Office for South Vietnam (COSVN), led by representatives from the North. But the early success of the VC did not come from northern support. It came from two factors: the growing ineptitude of Diem's regime and the presence of the United States.

Vietnamese culture has long tended toward xenophobia and racism. Diem was caught in a dilemma. If he received no support from the United States, he would not have enough money to pay the thousands of officials in his government. His army—the Army of the Republic of Vietnam (ARVN, pronounced ''Arvin'' by Americans)—would not be well trained in the new weaponry supplied by Washington. In other words, if Diem did not embrace America's offer of friendship, his regime would be in trouble.

On the other hand, if Diem accepted American support, he would appear to his own people like a flunky of the Americans, the white-skinned Westerners. He would seem a disgraceful puppet, a successor to those countrymen who had once served France.

Diem's quandary represented one of the great tragedies in this long war. The motives of the United States were relatively pure. America merely wanted to "help" and get out. But every type of assistance America provided South Vietnam hurt as well as helped. America's mere touch was poisonous. The Vietnamese had learned to loathe the French. They had no desire for another colonial master. The United States could not help but look like another France, another Western imperialist.

Once the VC insurgency began, Diem could not succeed without the United States. With its aid, he almost inevitably had to fail.

John Adams once reputedly said that the American Revolution did not begin in 1775 at Lexington and Concord; it began years earlier, in the "hearts and minds" of the American colonists.[5] Adams's phrase well describes one aspect of any civil disturbance. To succeed, a would-be government must try to reach both the hearts and the minds of its people. That was the goal of the Vietcong.

The VC put most of their focus on the rural villagers, who in 1963 made up about eighty-five percent of South Vietnam's population. Mao Zedong had once said that his revolutionaries should be like fish swimming inside the water of the peasantry. VC cadres constantly reminded new recruits of the three "withs": The VC should *eat with, work with,* and *live with* the peasants. Diem's government was made up of city folk—many of them Catholics—and they seemed quite "foreign" to most Vietnamese peasants. A VC organizer, living inside a peasant hamlet—assisting the farmers in the fields, respectful toward local customs and local women—not only seemed like one of them but generally was.

But one should not romanticize the Vietcong. As a group, they were not "good guys." They were capable of acts of extraordinary violence.

The Vietcong would choose a village. They would arrive at the hamlet and explain to the villagers that Diem's "outsider" government was repellent and must be overthrown. Then they often turned on the leader, the chief, of that village. If the man was known to be corrupt, the VC cadres would cruelly slaughter him. While the hamlet's population was forced to watch, the cadres disemboweled the chief or cut off his head; then they would do the same to his wife and his children. On the other hand, if the village had a *good* and independent chief who might give the VC any opposition, they often killed him anyway. By such acts they showed their raw power and their determination.

Diem and his government were virtually powerless to do anything about such activities. Their influence in rural areas was often minimal at best. Part of the problem was that in military matters Diem had to depend on his army, the ARVN, and it was a weak reed.

Good soldiers are not merely young men—or women—with weapons. They generally are well trained, well disciplined, and well led. Some ARVN troops were brave soldiers; some of their officers were excellent commanders. But those were the exception. ARVN soldiers tended to avoid battle if they could and, if they couldn't, to retreat with astonishing regularity.

Why was this? Since they derived from the same stock as the Vietcong, why did the ARVN soldiers evade fighting while the cadres fought with such consistent ferocity? The answer seems to lie in two elements: loyalty and leadership.

Diem was terrified of being overthrown by a coup. He created his government and his army through contacts, payoffs, and fear. If you were ambitious in the South Vietnamese military, you quickly learned that the path to success lay in Saigon, not out in the field. High-ranking officers preferred to stay in Saigon, where they could polish the ripest apples, rather than leave town. If you were outside the watchful eye of Diem, he suspected you might be plotting something; so it seemed prudent to stay in the capital. Furthermore, it was important always to make Diem look good. If you actually fought a battle and won a major victory, you might become a rival of Diem's, which was dangerous—his jails were filled with potential rivals. Or, equally bad, you might lose the battle. If that occurred, you looked incompetent or, worse, possibly traitorous. Thus it seemed much wiser to avoid fighting. Later in the war the Americans practiced "search and destroy" missions; GIs contemptuously called the ARVN tactic "seek and evade."

The cautious attitude of ARVN's officers fed on itself. Desertion was common in ARVN units, even when they were not in battle. In one unit, for example, sixty-seven percent of the men were AWOL (absent without leave). Such statistics reflected social and political problems in South Vietnam; they also meant that the ARVN was a weak army, militarily undependable.

There was also the matter of corruption in the ARVN. The members of some units sold their equipment, including their new American weapons, to the VC for cash. They would also accept bribes to leave the VC alone. In one of the most remarkable examples of graft in the ARVN, some artillery batteries refused to provide fire support to their own infantry unless they were first bribed. Then there was the practice of inflating the numbers of soldiers on a unit's rolls. Since each military unit was paid according to the number of men it had, a greedy officer could get rich padding his numbers. A particular battalion was collecting pay for 582 men when it actually had only 150. One can imagine the surprise of some general who sent that battalion into battle, expecting almost six hundred fighters and getting a quarter of that number.

The cavalier attitude toward battle of so many of the ARVN officers was hardly surprising. An army's officers need to feel some sense of commitment or loyalty to something. It was almost impossible to feel a strong devotion to Diem's regime. It has to be remembered that South Vietnam was not a *nation*, and, despite some words on the Geneva Accords, it could hardly be considered a *country*. Nor did Diem himself have the kind of charisma that might create emotional ties.

The average ARVN soldier had great potential. The success of the VC proved that. But he was badly led and often confused. His government never saw it necessary to indoctrinate him, to inspire him, as the VC cadres did with their new recruits. The ARVN soldier tended to be a badly educated, wretchedly paid peasant far from home, frightened and listless in his ill-fitting uniform. Sometimes, when sent on operations, he acted vilely. He raped village women, he ransacked huts, he opened fire indiscriminately on his own people. Such actions usually were done by ARVN soldiers in the worse-led units, but these incidents occurred all too frequently. Yet when ARVN troops were well trained and were led by good officers, they fought bravely and without complaint; they performed feats of great endurance. The flaws in the ARVN were not the fault of its average soldier. The blame lay with its leaders.

The American military became involved in Vietnam by small increments, one step at a time. This process began when Eisenhower sent three hundred soldiers to Vietnam to advise the ARVN how to organize and fight.

"Ike" Eisenhower was by nature a conservative, cautious man. He projected, not entirely accidentally, an image of beaming decency—a vaguely bumbling "nice guy," everyone's favorite relative. (A shrewd advertising man, faced with promoting a new kitchen cleanser, stamped a close facsimile of Ike on the front of the bottle and called the new product "Mr. Clean." It sold extremely well.) A famous political button in 1952 declared, "I like Ike." Most people did.

The late 1950s—the years of Eisenhower's presidency—were the time of beatniks and Elvis, of Marilyn Monroe and Martin Luther King, Jr., of Mickey Mantle and the Mickey Mouse Club, of the hula hoop, of 3D movies, of the birth of McDonald's hamburgers and the death of Frank Lloyd Wright, of white bucks and blue suede shoes, of Doris Day. In the complex nation that was America in the 1950s, no single person or thing could represent the entire culture. But Eisenhower came as close as anyone to personifying the era. He was, as people said, as American as apple pie—for good or ill.

Late in the decade Ike's health began to fade. He had two major heart attacks, either of which might have killed him, and his doctors told him to take it easy. He painted—rather well, actually—and he played a great deal of golf. Golf is a perfectly good sport and painting

An American adviser (right) trains a South Vietnamese rifle squad. The U.S. military first became involved in Vietnam in the late 1950s, when several hundred advisers were sent.

is a fine hobby, but they both smacked a bit of the sedentary, of the activities of a rather old man in dubious health, a person who was a bit . . . feeble.

In 1960 a young senator from Massachusetts, John F. Kennedy, ran for the presidency. His campaign emphasized not so much his youth—he didn't want to seem too immature to face the Russians—as his "vigor." He said he wanted to "get the country going again," implying that it had become tired and too cautious under Eisenhower and his Republican administration, a nation with hardened arteries. Kennedy and his team promised energy and action. Kennedy called his approach the New Frontier. The phrase had little concrete meaning; it was knowingly filched from Franklin D. Roosevelt's New Deal, the range of social programs introduced by that president in the 1930s. The New Frontier was intended to suggest that Kennedy and his fellow Democrats were offering an exciting and challenging new product, whose chief value was that it was different from the apparent lethargy of the last years of Eisenhower.

The election of 1960 was close, but Jack Kennedy defeated his Republican rival, Eisenhower's vice president, Richard Nixon. In January 1961, Eisenhower's torch was passed to Kennedy's "new generation."

When President Kennedy entered office in January 1961, he felt confident. He was sure he could handle the intricate problems of the Cold War. He and his administration were bright, they were young, and they had a plan.

Eisenhower, they felt, had allowed America to become muscle-bound with nuclear power. Ike had wanted to balance the budget; he had refused to spend huge sums of money on a gigantic military if he could find some alternative. One of his Cabinet members had said it best: They had wanted "more bang for the buck." Nuclear weapons seemed the most efficient way to counter what they saw as the only real danger to the United States—the Soviet Union.

Soviet leader Joseph Stalin's death in 1953 had been followed by several years of bureaucratic infighting. Then a sly, tough little man named Nikita Khrushchev grasped the reins of power. He was filled with bombast and bluster, strutting across the world's stage like an operatic character, like a cartoon dictator. He said that Communism would "bury" the American system. Was that meant as mere political rhetoric, or even poetic imagery—or was it a distinct threat? Khrushchev might not be quite as ruthless a killer as Joseph Stalin, but the new head of the Soviet Union was clearly a gambler and might therefore be dangerous.

Eisenhower's government had faced Khrushchev with a policy of "massive retaliation," which promised nuclear war if the Soviets became too aggressive. President Kennedy was unsatisfied with this situation. In his view, Eisenhower's policies had made the United States unable to deal with small problems that did not lend themselves to threats of "massive retaliation." Kennedy called for a new policy called "flexible response."

According to Kennedy's new plans, America would build up its *entire* military, not just its nuclear capacity. Then, if an opportunity—or a necessity—arose, the United States could step in. If Russia invaded Western Europe, the United States could still use its nuclear weapons; but if a "brushfire war" started in some distant land, America could deal with that, too.

"Let the word go forth," Kennedy announced as he took his oath of office, "to friend and foe alike that the torch has been passed to a new generation." And he promised: "To those peoples in the huts and villages of half the globe . . . we pledge our best efforts."[6]

He was not thinking of Vietnam, but the words would later seem prophetic.

John Kennedy's first great adversary, meanwhile, was Nikita Khrushchev. The Soviet premier had just made his own promise: Russia, Khrushchev announced, would support "wars of liberation" anywhere in the globe. One could assume from these words that the Soviets might aid rebels and their rebellions throughout Africa and Asia—perhaps in South Vietnam.

During Kennedy's first two years in office, he, like all presidents, had a few failures and some successes. In the eyes of most people, his greatest success came during the Cuban missile crisis in 1962. He forced Khrushchev to withdraw a packet of missiles from Fidel Castro's Cuba. The method he used was important. During a one-week period in October 1962, Kennedy carefully cranked up the level of military threats against Russia. Each move, each step forward, was as calculated as a chess game. The whole point was to intimidate his adversaries so that they would back down.

During the euphoria that followed the missile crisis, the members of Kennedy's administration felt the glow of popular congratulations. They were heroes. As Secretary of State Dean Rusk said, they had been eyeball-to-eyeball with the other fellow—and he had blinked. They had accomplished this with a combination of toughness and intelligence. They felt they now knew how to solve international problems anywhere—including Vietnam.

In South Vietnam things were not going as well. Under Kennedy the United States increased its military support of Diem. From Eisenhower's 300 military advisers, Kennedy gradually approved more and more men—until, by November 1963, the United States had 16,000 military advisers in Vietnam. America also sent the ARVN more modern military equipment, especially helicopters and armored personnel carriers (APCs).

For a while this infusion of new equipment seemed to help Diem's army. Throughout the South the VC were knocked backward. Then the same old pattern repeated itself. The Vietcong, after a bit, learned how these new things worked, and they adapted. It was this ability to adapt that made the Vietcong so successful. If the ARVN increased its size, so would its enemies. If the ARVN got new weapons or tactics, the VC learned to counter them. Slowly the VC took over more and more of South Vietnam.

By 1963, Diem's most glaring problem had become clear. It was his brother Nhu.

Ngo Dinh Nhu was in charge of South Vietnam's police, responsible for searching out and eliminating traitors. But "treason" can be a fuzzy word, especially in a society in turmoil. Nhu defined treason as virtually any opposition to Diem. Vietnamese newsmen who dared to write critical articles found themselves in one of Nhu's "tiger cages," hideous prison cells where prisoners were starved and often tortured to death. Even normal political opponents of Diem ended up in prison—or dead. Nhu's police reputedly eliminated tens of thousands of Vietnamese. Nhu himself began to crack under the strain. Perhaps to calm himself, he started to take opium—and he became addicted. The drug started to wear him down, to shatter his stability. He became increasingly manic— and dangerous.

Then, to make matters worse, a religious controversy exploded. Diem's government had long offered special benefits to fellow Catholics. Eventually the Buddhists grew impatient.

Buddhism, like most religions, has many forms, but

*In 1963, the suicides of several Buddhist monks
mobilized opposition to Diem's rule. News photos
such as this one, capturing the suicide of one
monk, shocked world opinion and focused new
attention on the situation in Vietnam.*

it contains one constant: Its central philosophy involves the renunciation of property. All materials things, all matters of the world, are considered mere vanity. A bonze is someone who gives up everything and becomes devoted to the worship of Buddha. In May 1963 the bonzes of the city of Hue were enraged when Diem refused to allow them to fly Buddha's flag on the anniversary of his birthday. (This was approximately equivalent to having the U.S. government cancel Christmas celebrations in New York.) There were protests in Hue. Diem's soldiers, sent there, opened fire on a crowd, killing nine.

As a protest, an elderly bonze publicly burned himself to death. Other bonzes followed. Such acts mobilized opposition to Diem's rule. By September many of South Vietnam's cities were in chaos. Had Diem lost the Mandate of Heaven? It seemed so.

A handful of Diem's generals began to plot against him and Nhu. But they had to be extremely cautious. If Nhu's police discovered their plans, their fate in his torture chambers would have been quite unpleasant. They asked America's representatives in Saigon to back them.

In Washington, John Kennedy was uncertain what to do. If Diem would only promise to rid himself of Nhu, then Kennedy would continue to support him. If not, then . . .

Diem refused to even listen to the not-so-subtle suggestions that he drop his brother from his government. And so his fate was sealed. Kennedy's government turned its back on Diem.

On November 1, 1963, Diem was overthrown by half a dozen frightened generals. He and his brother Nhu were then murdered.

The history of South Vietnam was about to change.

THE NEXT STEP

On November 22, 1963—three weeks after Diem's death—John F. Kennedy was assassinated in Dallas. Since then, people have debated whether or not Kennedy would have taken America deeper into war in Vietnam. Those who say that he would not have done so note his growing doubts about America's involvement in that distant land and point out that Kennedy did not entirely trust the judgment of his military advisers. Kennedy believed that many of them felt a kind of knee-jerk support for war. He considered them good professionals, but he suspected that their views were too narrow. He and his administration thought it important to control the Pentagon.

On the other hand, by the time of Kennedy's death, the United States, with 16,000 military advisers in Vietnam, was deeply committed to the war. The presence of these Americans was a fact that could not be ignored. If Kennedy withdrew them and South Vietnam fell to the Vietcong, he—and the entire Democratic party—would have been open to the same sort of attacks that Truman had suffered when Mao took over China. It seems doubtful Kennedy would have chanced this. Besides, after the missile crisis, he and his team felt cocky about their abilities.

Then came the assassination—and Lyndon Johnson was president.

President Lyndon Johnson was not always a nice man. He could be a shouting bully to his staff, shredding their egos with sneering sarcasm. He was coarse and capable of great vulgarity; he swore constantly and told filthy ethnic jokes. But he had an ambition: to be remembered as the greatest president in America's history. To achieve that goal he developed a program he called the Great Society. Its goals were to end poverty in America, eliminating the vast pockets of desperately poor people across the land; provide a good education for every young American, from preschool (Project Head Start) through college; and ensure decent medical care for every citizen. It was a wonderful dream. He would, in fact, accomplish a surprising amount of it. Johnson had been in office only a few months when major legislation began to pour out of Congress. To achieve the fullness of the Great Society, however, Johnson wanted to make sure he won the election of November 1964 in a landslide. To accomplish that, he was determined to make himself seem like a "peace" president. The situation in Vietnam was too complicated—a minefield for an ambitious presidential candidate like Johnson. He preferred that voters not think too much or too deeply about Vietnam. He seldom spoke about it during his campaign.

Johnson's rival that year was the Republican nominee Barry Goldwater, a senator from Arizona. Goldwater, a pleasant, honest, likable man, often made foolish, tough-sounding statements. He reputedly once joked that one solution to the Cold War was to fling an atomic bomb into the men's room of the Kremlin. This statement, if ever actually uttered, was simply a jest, but he did seem a bit trigger-happy to many Americans. That impression made Johnson happy, for it made him seem sane and peaceful. The only thing he had to worry about was that an incident might occur somewhere—especially in Vietnam—where he might be made to look weak. He wanted to seem like a man of peace, *not* a weakling.

Then something happened in the waters of the Tonkin Gulf, off North Vietnam.

The background to the Tonkin Gulf incident is complex—and still a matter of debate. The story began with a highly secret operation, supervised by the CIA, called OPLAN 34A. Small speedboats carrying South Vietnamese raiders headed up the coast of South Vietnam, past the DMZ, and moved in toward shore where they attacked coastal installations. The American government was also running, simultaneously, an overlapping operation called Desoto. Naval destroyers carrying highly technical equipment sailed not far off the coast of North Vietnam on spying missions. One of these destroyers was the U.S.S. *Maddox*.

On July 31, 1964, four small South Vietnamese patrol boats, part of the CIA's OPLAN 34A, bombarded the coast of North Vietnam about 50 miles (80 kilometers) from the Red River delta in Tonkin. A few miles away steamed the *Maddox*. Nor surprisingly, the North Vietnamese believed that the *Maddox* was part of the operation and sent out some Soviet-built PT boats to attack the destroyer. Although little came of the PT-boat assault on the *Maddox*, Johnson felt he could not, in the middle of his campaign against Goldwater, allow himself to appear cowardly. So a second destroyer, the U.S.S. *Turner Joy,* was sent to accompany the *Maddox.*

One night several days later, the crews of the two destroyers came to the conclusion that they were being fired on by North Vietnamese PT boats. The evidence seems to indicate that the apparent "attack" was, in fact, merely a misreading of some confusing sonar and radar signals. Yet whether or not the *Maddox* and the *Turner Joy* were actually fired on this time, the presumed "attack" had major consequences.

Almost within minutes of this second "attack," Lyndon Johnson was informed. He made two decisions. He ordered an immediate retaliatory bombing raid of some North Vietnamese torpedo-boat bases, and he asked Congress to support this action—and any *similar actions* in the future.

Three days later both houses of Congress met and almost unanimously voted for the Tonkin Gulf Resolution. It authorized the president "to take all necessary measures to repel any armed attack against the forces of the United States and to prevent further aggression."[7] This phrase of the resolution gave the White House immense power and helped to drag the United States much deeper into the war in Southeast Asia. How could one "prevent further aggression" unless one destroyed the capability of the other side to fight? How could one do that unless both the VC *and* the NVA (the North Vietnamese Army) were eliminated? The American government would wrestle with that quandary for the next nine years.

President Johnson had received congressional permission to expand the war. But he preferred not to do so. Despite the Tonkin Gulf incidents and the follow-up bombing raid, Johnson, with the election just a few weeks away, still wanted to present himself to the voters as a man of peace. In fact, Johnson really was unenthusiastic about war. Many members of his administration were pressing him to take firmer action against North Vietnam. He resisted. His focus was still on his Great Society. He well knew that a war with North Vietnam might sidetrack America from his goals.

But, after August 1964, he knew that if he ever changed his mind about Vietnam, the Tonkin Gulf Resolution justified whatever action he might decide to take; it was a "functional equivalent" to a declaration of war.

Meanwhile, during 1964, political events in Saigon had gone haywire. Politics there had become very personal. One owed loyalty to a man, not a party or a system or an idea. When Diem was murdered, his successors, the junta of generals, began to replace his people with their own followers. In Saigon and out in the provinces the result was political turmoil; in the army it was almost as bad. Meanwhile, the members of the junta wrestled with one another. One of them would grab the leadership of South Vietnam; then he would be ousted and another would take his place. Each time this happened, the man at the top put some of his own followers in critical positions. The result, inevitably, was chaos. The Vietcong, of course, were pleased at these developments—and took advantage of them.

Hanoi decided in 1964 to shift to an offensive strategy. Representatives from the North were sent down to take over command of all Communist military planning in the South. By April 1964 the VC began to operate in larger units. In the past, their biggest forces had run to about two or three hundred people. Now the VC started carrying out regiment-sized operations, involving a thousand soldiers or more. The fighting between the VC and the ARVN became fiercer. An American adviser noted: "Up to now, this war has been a patient cat-and-mouse game. Now it is becoming lions against tigers."[8]

For the Communists this had two results. Larger VC units meant more supplies and larger, more complicated weapons. It also meant heavier Vietcong losses. These two factors—the need for more supplies and more soldiers—led to an important new development in the war, the expansion of the Ho Chi Minh Trail.

The so-called Ho Chi Minh Trail was not a road. It was hardly even a trail. The phrase referred to the major land-route supply line between North and South Vietnam.

People and matériel could come from the North by several routes. They could, for example, travel from North Vietnam by water. They could be transported in small boats, moving down the coastline and slipping after dark onto some prearranged beach. Or larger vessels could sail them all the way past Saigon, perhaps as far as Cambodia; then they could press inland toward their objective in South Vietnam. After the war was over, North Vietnamese officials suggested that more than half the supplies had gone by water.

During the war, however, the chief focus of America's concern was the land route between North and South Vietnam, the Ho Chi Minh Trail. The DMZ completely split the two sections of Vietnam, running from the Tonkin Gulf to the mountains. Those wanting to move supplies could try to slip across the DMZ; but the ARVN was becoming increasingly wary, and this route grew more dangerous with each passing month.

Another way to move matériel was to carry it west from North Vietnam over the mountains into Laos and, using the mountain range as a shield to hide behind, slide down past the DMZ. Then one could either sneak

directly into the northern part of South Vietnam or move farther south, through Cambodia, and enter the South not far from Saigon. It was this long pathway that was called the Ho Chi Minh Trail.

Men and equipment had filtered down this route since the beginning of the conflict. The regroupees who had returned home in 1959 had often come this way. Now, in 1964, this trail became more significant—and more well traveled.

The beginning of the trail, in North Vietnam, was in Hanoi. It headed south inside North Vietnam to a place not even on the map—just a clearing in the jungle not far from the Laotian border that was called Ho Village. Then it moved westward into Laos.

By 1964 most of the regroupees had already departed; now, those who started down the trail were increasingly North Vietnamese who knew they were leaving home for a very long time. These small, thin men, carrying their weapons and 60-pound (27-kilogram) packs, stepped off and began their two-month journey. Each one was embarked on an awesome trek requiring incredible fortitude. Most American soldiers who carried that much equipment would become tired after a few hours, exhausted after several days. But, amazingly, day after day the North Vietnamese moved southward. They waded across rushing rivers and streams. They struggled their way up and down the sides of the mountains. They

U.S. soldiers walking along part of the Ho Chi Minh Trail. The Vietcong had placed log steps at one-stride intervals in this section of the trail.

[79]

walked about fourteen hours a day. On their feet they wore simple sandals made of strips taken from old tires. These shoes never rotted, as regulation U.S. Army boots would have done.

When they started out each morning, they had a goal to reach. Normally, a liaison man who knew the way to that evening's stopover led them, leaving them the next morning and returning to escort the next group. Later on, the trail became more clearly marked and was widened and made firm enough to handle heavily laden trucks. But in these early years, it was not a road; it was a network of paths and tracks in the jungle. The men moved secretly; they didn't want to be spotted from the air. The jungle growth was thick. One could walk for many miles beneath the canopy of leaves and never see the sun—nor be seen by any watchful planes. To confuse their enemies, the North Vietnamese often used a particular path only a single time and then left it abandoned. Within a week or two the jungle reclaimed it.

The trek south was difficult for the men who made it, but they and the supplies had to get through for their cause to stand a chance against the military might of America. During the war a wry tale made the rounds of the South. It involved a fictional North Vietnamese who was drafted into his army, given a single heavy mortar round, and sent southward. For two long, horrible months he struggled over craggy mountains carrying his burden. He caught diseases in the jungles and lost weight. He nearly drowned in a flooding river. He was attacked by animals along the way, by poisonous snakes and man-eating tigers. He huddled in the monsoon rains and picked leeches off his face. He was constantly terrified of American bombers flying overhead. Finally he arrived at his destination in South Vietnam. Just as he got there, a battle began. He staggered forward with his burden, the mortar shell. A Vietcong soldier grabbed it from his trembling hands, popped it in a mortar, shot it at the enemy, then turned to him and said, "Go back for another." The story, although a bit stretched, told a central truth—the Ho Chi Minh supply line was crucial.

Yet it would be a mistake to exaggerate the amount of supplies coming down the trail at this time. Almost all the weapons used by the Vietcong in 1964 were old French items or, increasingly, American weapons that the VC bought, captured, or stole from the ARVN. The Americans, however, were anxious to halt what they called "the flow of supplies from the North."

During its long war with North Vietnam, the American military tried all sorts of techniques to stop this movement of men and supplies. If they could find the trail, the Americans believed, they could bomb it into uselessness. But finding it was difficult. The vast canopy of jungle growth prevented easy sighting from the air. So the Americans tried other things.

They sent small units of Special Forces troops (Green Berets) into the mountains to work with the montagnards—to make deals with certain tribes, to arm them with modern weapons, and to use them to pinpoint the hidden paths that made up the trail. American intelligence officers interrogated prisoners about the position of the trail. American pilots flew scout planes to search for it. American military planners became so frustrated that they even developed something they called a "sniffer" plane, which would fly slowly over the tops of the trees and "sniff" the air. If the plane's mechanical device picked up the scent of ammonia—a chief ingredient in urine—it was assumed that a band of enemy soldiers might be lurking—and, presumably, urinating—below. The United States would immediately send bombers to that spot and bomb it. There is no record of any successes in the operations of the "sniffer" plane. Perhaps some North Vietnamese were killed, but most likely watering holes used by unsuspecting animals would have been the primary targets of the bombers.

The Ho Chi Minh Trail would eventually cause the war in Vietnam to evolve into an Indochina war. Because of the trail, the North Vietnamese felt they needed to control the eastern half of Laos. They therefore supported a Laotian Communist organization that called itself the Pathet Lao. In return, the Pathet Lao gave them support inside the eastern Laotian provinces. (In a sense Eisenhower was right. By 1964, part of Laos had fallen, like a domino, to the Communists.)

The Green Berets were under orders not to enter either Laos or Cambodia; in the jungle, however, one could not see precisely where a country's borders were. Green Beret "A teams," as they were called, casually slipped back and forth across the borders looking for the enemy and his trail.

More important than a handful of A teams was the bombing. Early in the war American planes began to bomb the portion of Laos where the trail was. By the end of the war the Pentagon calculated that they had dropped more than twice as much bomb tonnage on the jungles of Laos than had been dropped on both Japan and Germany during World War II.

John Kennedy had noted the importance of the trail. "No matter what goes wrong," he had said, "or whose fault it really is, the argument will be that the Communists have stepped up their infiltration and we can't win unless we hit the North. Those trails are a built-in excuse for failure, and a built-in argument for escalation."[9] It was a remarkably prophetic statement. When President Kennedy made that remark, the war still had more than ten years to go. Yet much of the rest of it would revolve in one way or another around the matter of the Ho Chi Minh Trail—and the seeming necessity of "interdicting" it (that is, cutting it and preventing its use). Perhaps part of the problem lay in its very name. A "trail" sounds like a specific, clearly defined road. Military experts are taught to "interdict" an enemy's roads. It was hard to imagine a road that bombers could not destroy. Yet that was the case. The trail was difficult to find. And, even if bombed, a dirt path is easily repaired.

Late in 1964 the war in South Vietnam moved another step forward. Three months after the events in the Tonkin Gulf, the Vietcong struck. Since the beginning of their war with South Vietnam, the VC had avoided direct conflict with American troops. When Americans were killed, it was usually because they were "advisers" with an ARVN unit that had come under attack.

Now, for the first time, the VC went out of their way to hit Americans. During the last weeks of 1964 and early 1965, they attacked a U.S. air base, blew up a Saigon hotel used by American soldiers, and dropped mortar shells on a U.S. Army barracks.

Johnson was angry, and—with the American election over and with a landslide victory in his back pocket— he no longer felt any necessity to hesitate. He ordered a series of bombing attacks on the North. Almost immediately, the Soviet Union promised to send aid to North Vietnam. Up to this moment, Hanoi's chief source of outside support had been China. Now the Russians were in the picture.

A civil war inside an impoverished Southeast Asian nation had come to involve the two greatest military forces in the history of the world, the United States and the Soviet Union.

By March 1965 the North Vietnamese had 6,000 soldiers in the South. Officially, they referred to themselves as the People's Army of Viet Nam (PAVN). Americans, however, called them the North Vietnamese Army—the NVA. Now three Vietnamese armies were fighting in the South: the ARVN, the VC, and the NVA. The United States also had more than 20,000 American soldiers stationed there, most of them military advisers.

Up to 1965, only 137 Americans had been killed in this war, which had already been going on for six years. While he lived, John Kennedy had written a personal note to the family of each serviceman killed in Indochina. Although it was a somber, unpleasant task, it did not take too much of his time. But now the mechanism for an expanded war was in place.

A crew of American soldiers pulls survivors from the wreckage of a U.S. Army barracks in Qui Nhon, South Vietnam, after a Vietcong attack. This and similar attacks marked a change in tactics for the Vietcong.

AMERICA GOES
TO WAR

By early 1965 it appeared that if the United States did
not become militarily involved, and soon, South Vietnam would shortly fall to the Communists. The Vietcong were increasing their efforts, and they were start-
ing to attack American installations. In addition, the NVA
was entering the war in a noticeable way. Saigon was
collapsing into a political dew; the ARVN inevitably was
following suit.

The Tonkin Gulf Resolution gave Lyndon Johnson
congressional backing for U.S. military action. Furthermore, he was finally ready to order his war machine into
battle. He was deeply angry at the North Vietnamese
and the VC, and his fury was replacing his previous
caution. He decided on a *program* of regular bombing
attacks on the North. He was not going to send pilots
across the DMZ merely in retaliation for some VC action. His new plan was that bombing was going to gradually increase in intensity and continue until the North
Vietnamese pulled out of South Vietnam.

Washington called this new operation Rolling Thunder. The bombing began in March 1965 and continued for three years. It was designed to punish North Vietnam for supporting the VC and to interdict supplies that might otherwise find their way down the Ho Chi Minh Trail.

Rolling Thunder never succeeded. The planes did destroy large amounts of military matériel, but Chinese and Soviet aid more than made up for any North Vietnamese losses. Nor did the planes eliminate the trail itself. North Vietnam soon had 300,000 people working full-time building and repairing the trail and another 200,000 working on it part-time. In fact, during the three years of Rolling Thunder the trail actually grew more sophisticated.

During the war in Vietnam, Americans flew their bombing missions from many air bases. Some came from Guam and others from the Philippines and Thailand; still others came from the decks of U.S. aircraft carriers in the waters off Southeast Asia. But every mile a plane flew used a certain amount of fuel, and fuel has weight. So do bombs. The mathematics of air power is easy: The farther a plane flies, the more fuel it has to carry— and the fewer bombs it can drop. To increase a bomber's effectiveness by having it carry more bombs on every mission, the plane must fly less distance; it is that simple. Air force analysts advised the Pentagon that, if North Vietnam was the target, it would be most efficient to build or enlarge airfields not too far south of the DMZ. Planes would not have to fly very far before they were at their targets and thus could carry more bombs.

America began to build air bases throughout South Vietnam. Each airfield altered the war—and South Vietnam—by a certain amount. One example was the air base at Da Nang.

Da Nang was a tired old port city when the war started. It had been an import-export town, as well as a fishing village, for centuries before the French had arrived in the nineteenth century. The French had added some wharves and piers, built dozens of new warehouses, and paved some roads, and the population of the city increased accordingly. But Da Nang never became an attractive or interesting place—just a rather dirty, crowded harbor town.

During Diem's regime his air force expanded Da Nang's small airport, just outside the city, and brought in a few small jets. Then, in 1965, the United States Air Force came. Its needs were massive. It would use the airfield for medium-sized bombers, which used huge amounts of fuel and carried many bombs. Each plane would need to be repaired frequently, and this meant hangars where repair crews could work. It meant supply warehouses for the storage of spare parts and equipment of every type.

Most complicated of all, American engineers needed to expand and extend the runways. A large jet, fully loaded, requires almost 2 miles (3 kilometers) of runway to take off. Each runway must be wide. There must be parallel runways and side runways where planes can taxi. The tarmac (forming the runways) must be able to withstand the great impact of a landing bomber. An airfield, therefore, must sit atop many feet of support material. Here again the problem is mathematical. Multiply the length of the air base by its width, then multiply that answer by its depth below the ground. The result equals how much material the United States needed to ship to Da Nang to build the airfield.

Americans imported enough concrete and asphalt to cover Rhode Island. They also had to bring in huge pieces of equipment: excavators, graders, bulldozers, backhoes, trucks of every variety. And the engineers discovered even before they began that the harbor of Da Nang was not deep enough to allow passage of the huge tankers and freighters that would bring the equipment to build the airfield. So they had to dredge out the harbor. Only a few dredging machines in the entire world were big enough to do the job. These monstrous machines had to be brought in pieces slowly across the Pacific and then erected inside the harbor and put to work.

The engineers also realized that the roads between the harbor and the airfield were not strong enough to sustain the weight of the convoys of heavy trucks that would drive back and forth. So they had to improve the roads, which meant more concrete and asphalt and equipment.

And they needed manpower. They needed crews of technicians to repair the planes. They needed supply sergeants to watch over and distribute the parts for the planes. And they needed pilots, of course. These men had to sleep, so they required barracks. They had to eat, so they needed mess halls. Some of them would become sick occasionally, so they needed infirmaries and hospital facilities. This meant nurses. And the nurses needed separate barracks.

Every single one of these Americans was far from home and would be lonely and bored. South Vietnam was very "foreign" to most Americans. The Vietnamese language was extremely difficult to learn, the population was not especially accommodating, and the weather was frightful. Half the year it was dry and an orange dust swirled in the air. The other half it rained, and it rained; things mildewed easily, and everything smelled strange to American nostrils. Almost every day, whether it was sunny or rainy, it was hot.

The United States did not want its military forces

to become too unhappy. This might reduce their morale—which is an important commodity. To compensate the Americans for their discomfort, their government attempted to make their tour in Vietnam, which was designated to be precisely 365 days long, as much like "home" as it could.

The military built movie theaters, bowling alleys, and basketball courts. They set up PXs where military personnel could purchase—at excellent prices—liquor, cameras, watches, toiletries, even lingerie. At the mess halls—and, later, even out in the field where the fighting soldiers struggled to stay alive—the government tried to make sure they almost always got hot meals, often steak. In one incredible bit of American ingenuity (or gall), the military decided to provide their people with ice cream on a regular basis. South Vietnam did not have enough milk, sugar, or equipment to make the ice cream. All of these things had to be brought in from the United States—including massive refrigerator units.

Building the airfield in Da Nang was a major and important operation, but it was merely one of dozens of similar projects. All this American building, which preceded most of the fighting, had some unfortunate consequences.

Every army has a "tail"—those people who are necessary to an army but who do not fight. Movie projectionists are part of a tail. So are engineers and truck drivers and specialists in airplane maintenance. So are doctors and nurses and intelligence officers. So are photographers and supply sergeants. Their jobs are usually not romantic, yet they are important.

The American tail was about eighty-five percent of America's military force in South Vietnam. Even when the force reached its peak in 1968, with about 540,000 people, it had only about 70,000 actual *fighting* men, called "grunts" by American soldiers.

Their enemies outnumbered the "grunts." As Rolling Thunder got under way, the Vietcong numbered between 50,000 and 65,000 full-time (Main Force) soldiers and an additional 150,000 regional and local fighters who served at least part of the time. The NVA, moreover, was already increasing the 6,000 troops it had in South Vietnam. The numbers of the NVA grew precisely as the Americans increased their presence in Southeast Asia. The North could more than match the United States in its ability to put infantrymen in the field.

The first U.S. ground troops arrived in March 1965. They were a unit of marines sent to guard the Da Nang air base. They landed on a sandy beach near the seaport and ran tensely onto the sands with guns across their arms. They did not know what to expect; their reception must have been disorienting. Pretty young Vietnamese college women were waiting for them and smilingly placed garlands of flowers around their necks. When the marines clambered on their trucks and rode toward their destination, they drove beneath banners proclaiming in English, "Thanks to the U.S. government and people." This reception must have convinced many marines that this whole operation was going to be a piece of cake.

During the next few months these first American ground troops would be joined by tens of thousands of their comrades in all services, then hundreds of thousands. America was at war.

And the country was self-assured. Since 1945 the people of the United States had come to see themselves as invincible. America had always been a cheerful, optimistic nation. Perhaps it was the vast expanse of the country, the cheap land, the ready supplies of coal and iron and oil. They had stood up to Kaiser Bill in World War I and to Tojo and Hitler in World War II. They had refused to be unnerved by Stalin or Mao. Their military

*U.S. Marines scramble ashore at Da Nang in March
1965. They were sent to guard the air base there.*

might had made Khrushchev back down in the Cuban missile crisis. Who could stand up to them? Certainly not "a bunch of little yellow guys in black pajamas," as many soldiers described them.

To view the war simply as "a white man's war," as some observers did, is to overlook a clear fact. A large percentage of America's fighting force in Vietnam was African-American or Hispanic. These troops came to Vietnam feeling just as superior, just as confident, as their white Anglo-Saxon comrades. All of them tended to refer to Vietnamese, friend or foe, as "gooks" or "slopes" or "dinks." These words were ethnic slurs, of course, but they indicated a sense of *cultural* more than racial superiority. (It ought to be noted that many Vietnamese felt culturally superior to the American GIs. Self-respecting middle-class Vietnamese parents refused to allow their daughters to date Americans, who seemed loud, crude, and boorish.)

The confident American soldiers who arrived in Vietnam found that they had to fight many different wars—in swamps and mountains and jungles. The ARVN had previously divided South Vietnam into four military regions. From the DMZ south along the coast, including the cities of Hue and Da Nang, was I (pronounced "eye") Corps. Here the fighting was very fierce. Since I Corps was near the border, the NVA could reach it easily. Washington decided to place the sector under the marines since the area was crucial and the marines were an elite unit.

Farther south lay II Corps, much of it a region of hills and mountains called the Central Highlands. Most Vietnamese here lived along the coast, leaving the actual highlands to the VC and the NVA.

Below that was III Corps, which included Saigon and the area around it for 40 to 50 miles (about 65 to 80 kilometers). This area was fairly flat and filled with towns and cities of various sizes. The larger cities were mostly "secure" in the military sense, but many of the small towns and villages were controlled by the Vietcong. The most remarkable example was a place called Cu Chi.

The U.S. Army had a military base near the town of Cu Chi. So did the VC—but theirs was underground. Long before the Americans arrived, the VC began building a network of tunnels beneath the region. Eventually they had miles of them. They built living areas, hospitals, and storage dumps under the ground. Part of their tunnel system actually burrowed right beneath the U.S. base. At night the Vietcong would slip out and speak to the nearby villagers or fire on the Americans; then they would pop back down again. American troops eventually discovered some of the tunnels, but they did not discover the extent of them for years.

The southernmost section of South Vietnam, the Mekong Delta, was IV Corps. Here the fighting was complicated because of the intricate nature of the delta's rivers and canals. Small boats that patrolled the waters were often targets of VC snipers hidden in the lush undergrowth on either side. The Vietcong had controlled much of the delta since the days of the French.

The man responsible for America's military effort in South Vietnam was General William C. Westmoreland ("Westy"). He had been in charge since June 1964. He was tall, lean, and strikingly handsome. His leadership ability and character had made him first captain of cadets at West Point, the approximate equivalent of student-body president. He had gone on to serve commendably in America's prestigious 101st Airborne Division during World War II. Like many high-ranking officers, he lacked a sense of humor; but he was an intelligent and a profoundly moral individual.

When Westmoreland was a West Point cadet, he no doubt studied many military techniques. Some would have involved speed and dash: a Macedonian cavalry charge against the Persians, the tactics of Stonewall Jackson in the Shenandoah Valley. Others would have required a hedgehog patience—hunkering down in a defensive position, letting the enemy break himself in futile attacks. Still other strategies would have depended on using massive numbers of troops to control a territory and expanding outward from that base. Eisenhower did just that from his Normandy beachhead in 1944.

Westmoreland could use none of these. He was involved in a long campaign, not a single battle. Speed and dash might work fine on a single day, in a particular engagement, but by itself this tactic was useless against an enemy like the Vietcong. Nor would pure patience succeed. The United States could not depend on mere defense—that would give the initiative to the other side, which was precisely what they wanted. The VC (and soon, the NVA) were excellent at making quick strikes and then retreating into the night or the shadows beneath the trees. And the Americans never had enough troops to control the whole of South Vietnam.

General Westmoreland had to devise another strategy. He finally accepted the necessity of a plan that military experts call an attrition policy. In this plan the American military would actively seek out the enemy and kill as many as possible. It was based on the assumption that only a certain specific number of VC (and NVA) were involved in the war. If you killed enough of them, you destroyed their effectiveness. You would, of course, like to "win the hearts and minds" of the Vietnamese people, but this was not your primary goal. Killing the VC was.

The first problem was to find the enemy. American soldiers on the ground and pilots in the air began to look for the VC. Intelligence sources of every type were tapped. In November 1965 came the first major test, in a place called the Ia Drang Valley. A large group of NVA regulars were caught in this desolate valley not far from the border of Laos. Westmoreland ordered his 1st Cavalry Division to destroy them.

1st Cav, as it was called, was a new concept in war. It effectively used helicopters—435 of them. Some of these airships were huge and could carry large numbers of infantrymen. Others were gunships; they were small, maneuverable craft with machine guns and rockets attached to them. Still other helicopters were designed to pick up the wounded. All of 1st Cav's pilots were trained to work closely together. Due to its difficult terrain, the Ia Drang Valley seemed a perfect test for this new type of warfare. And it worked. 1st Cav killed a great many of the enemy.

Helicopters had both successes and failures in Vietnam. They were superb instruments of medical aid. It has been calculated that, because of them, a wounded American in Vietnam was no more than fifteen minutes from good medical help. Sometimes, as in the Ia Drang Valley, the helicopters helped win battles. But too much dependence on them may have hindered the U.S. war effort. Using helicopters sometimes allowed young American soldiers to wake up, eat breakfast, get into a helicopter, fly to a battle area, fight for a while, and return to base. The control of the land—and much more important, the people who lived on the land—was left to the enemy.

The result was occasional battlefield success but also a feeling of frustration among the soldiers. They often fought for the exact same turf in battle after battle, each time flying home to their bases knowing that they might be called back again to fight in the same place. This sort of war allowed no sense of victory or momentum.

*U.S. soldiers jump from an armored helicopter at
the start of a "search and destroy" mission.
Inset: General William C. Westmoreland, who headed
the U.S. military effort in Vietnam.*

[97]

America's war in Vietnam was many things, but the grunt's primary missions in Vietnam ("in-country," as he called it) involved searching for the enemy. Some of these actions involved small units—a company, perhaps, or even a platoon. But the largest ones—with names such as Cedar Falls, Junction City, Dewey Canyon, Apache Snow—often involved the sweeping movements of tens of thousands of ground troops. Cedar Falls was fairly typical.

In January 1967, Westmoreland sent 30,000 combat soldiers toward a region of South Vietnam referred to as the Iron Triangle. It was a Vietcong stronghold 60 square miles (155 square kilometers) in size. The most frustrating fact about the Iron Triangle was that it lay only 20 miles (32 kilometers) from Westmoreland's headquarters in Saigon. At the beginning of the Cedar Falls offensive, B-52s flew back and forth across the area, saturating its rice paddies and rubber plantations, its villages and jungles, with heavy bombs. Then came the ground troops who poured across the region. They found much evidence of Vietcong activities: leaflets, food stores, some weapons. They even sighted some actual VC, whom they blasted with intensive firepower, killing perhaps seven hundred or more. The Americans then removed the civilian population, brought in huge plows, and leveled the area, destroying its vegetation so that guerrillas would have nowhere to hide. They dynamited its tunnels and, as they were leaving, dropped more bombs on it. Yet even as the last American soldiers were pulling out, they noticed Vietcong guerrillas with AK-47s slipping back in.

Cedar Falls symbolized much of the war. Americans fought well in Vietnam from 1965 to 1968, almost always winning, almost never losing an engagement of any size. But in general the initiative lay with the enemy. When he chose to fight, battles took place. When he decided that the odds were too heavy against him, he merely slipped back into the jungle or even across the borders of Laos or Cambodia. It was a war without clear lines, with no simple territorial objectives. Westmoreland simply did not have enough manpower to take and defend all of South Vietnam. His only alternative, he concluded, was his policy of attrition.

How could you know you were winning a war of attrition? Because your goal was killing the enemy, your "victories" were measured by the number of their dead bodies you accumulated—that you *assumed*, since the enemy often secretly carried away their dead and wounded after a battle.

Each day, Westmoreland's headquarters announced that day's military activities. A young public information officer told reporters how many of the enemy had been killed or wounded in that day's, or that week's, engagements. To arrive at figures, Westmoreland's office asked his generals for reports; they asked their colonels, who asked their majors, and so on down the line to the lieutenants and sergeants.

Each pressed those below them to write up "good" reports that would make their superiors look good. The pressure to fudge the numbers of the body count was immense. A sergeant who wanted an R and R (that is, a "rest and recuperation" leave) might be inclined to boost the figures just a bit; a lieutenant who was considering making the military his career might add a few more bodies to appear successful. The accumulated exaggerations and lies worked their way upward. Reporters in Saigon quickly came to recognize the pattern and referred to the daily briefings at Westmoreland's headquarters as the "five o'clock follies." They laughed at the official body count figures. They felt obligated to report them, of course; but they often added their own doubts to the reports.

It has long been recognized that the "first casualty" of war is the truth.[10] Journalists know this. They are aware that governments, under war conditions, are not always strictly truthful. But the training of reporters, and generally their inclination, forces them to dig for factual accuracy. In Vietnam they inevitably began to see the entire military bureaucracy as involved in a giant cover-up of the truth. In a sense reporters began to see themselves as knights searching for the holy grail of Truth, and the army as the dragon. Not surprisingly, the military brass generally had the opposite reaction. The army viewed the reporters as enemies, or at least adversaries.

This conflict between the military and the press was hardly new. During the Civil War, General William Tecumseh Sherman, among others, spoke bitterly about the press. During World War II, General Douglas MacArthur openly and contemptuously manipulated reporters. What was different in Vietnam was not the attitude of the army; it was the *importance* of the press. Lyndon Johnson remained highly sensitive to the mood of the American people. Their support was important to his master plan, his Great Society program. The media were his pipeline to his constituents. Since the media could influence the public, for or against his programs, he wanted their support—in Vietnam as well as in the United States. And since reporters wanted war news, he wanted to give it to them. He wanted them, however, to publish only *his* version of the story. Any contrary opinion enraged him.

Johnson was caught in a bind. He felt he could not ignore the media, nor would he allow his army to do so. Yet he did not want reporters to do their jobs, to publish all the facts. The results were inevitable. Before long, news reporters talked of something they called "the credibility gap," the difference between the truth and the stories they were being told—in Saigon, at the Pentagon, even at the White House.

During 1965 the government of South Vietnam fell into the hands of a political-military coalition led by two men, Nguyen Cao Ky and Nguyen Van Thieu. Ky was a handsome, flashy individual who loved parading around in a bright blue air force flight suit and dark glasses. For more than a year he seemed to be in charge of things in South Vietnam, but he lacked the necessary subtlety, and perhaps ruthlessness, to remain atop such a cauldron. By 1967, Thieu had taken power. He would not relinquish it until 1975. Thieu ran his regime much as Diem had done. He made deals, he threatened or eliminated rivals, he bought off opponents. Given the extraordinary circumstances of his war-torn country, he proved a reasonably capable leader. But, although the problem were certainly not all Thieu's fault, during his regime South Vietnam seemed to implode.

The war had a variety of negative effects on Thieu's country. In 1961 the South was eighty-five percent rural. Five years later the United States actually had to import rice to feed the South Vietnamese. By 1968 more than half the population lived in urban centers, mostly huddled in overcrowded slums.

There was also an array of social problems. Prostitution skyrocketed. In Saigon there were eventually 56,000 *registered* prostitutes. (How many women prostituted themselves for food and did not register with their government cannot even be estimated.) Males also wanted to profit from the American prosperity. Construction jobs

Nguyen Van Thieu (left), with bodyguards, in 1973.

on American projects paid so well that garbage pickup in Saigon virtually ceased.

Crime was another growth industry in South Vietnam. Thievery was a profitable enterprise. Robbers and muggers worked the streets of every city, often preying on drunken GIs on R and R. Some thieves—often teenagers and even younger children—worked in gangs. Others acted individually or in pairs, riding their scooters through congested streets, trolling for likely targets whose watches or wallets they could steal.

The corruption of governmental officials and ARVN leaders, already bad, got worse. Food and medicine sent from the United States to be distributed to the Vietnamese population often ended up sidetracked and then sold for the private profit of members of the government. Inflation skyrocketed.

The larger the American military presence grew, the easier it was for the ARVN to do less. They retreated into military enclaves. Instead of Americans adding to ARVN's military force, therefore, they merely replaced it. To be sure, they could bring more military efficiency into the field and more firepower, but they found it difficult to destroy a foe they could hardly detect. The ARVN had had difficulties finding and fighting the VC; the Americans were even more befuddled. GIs spoke little or no Vietnamese, and they had no understanding of the subtleties of the culture. How could one ferret out the VC if they looked just like everyone else? Accidents were inevitable. American firepower sometimes hit innocent civilians.

All of these things made America's war in Vietnam as complicated and as "dirty" as France's war had been. The inflation and corruption wrought by the influx of American dollars were symptoms of America's war. They were not immediately recognized; they only grew slowly apparent over the next several years.

Yet it was also apparent that the U.S. troops made an important difference to the war. In March 1965, on the day the marines arrived, the Vietcong controlled almost half the population of South Vietnam, and the situation was tipping even further in the VC's favor. During the Vietcong's spring offensive, which began in February 1965, the ARVN was dissolving. The situation was critical. If the United States had not thrown in combat troops during 1965, it is likely that Saigon would have soon fallen.

These young American soldiers and marines who poured into South Vietnam in 1965 were healthy, patriotic, well trained, and well armed. Their discipline and their firepower made a difference. The Vietcong were stopped. The Americans even began to retake a few regions from the VC. The nightly body count, as repellent as it was, did indicate American successes.

There were also ominous signs. The numbers of Vietcong were not going down significantly. No matter how many of them the Americans killed, there seemed just as many, perhaps more. Also, intelligence reports showed clearly that North Vietnam was sending more NVA troops southward.

Westmoreland asked for reinforcements and was granted them. He needed as many men as he could get. The theory in the Pentagon was that after American troops defeated the enemy in a particular region, the Americans would move on and the ARVN soldiers could enter and control the area. American combat units, therefore, would have the opportunity to look elsewhere for the enemy, knowing that the territory they had turned over to the ARVN was "secure." Unfortunately, it did not work out so neatly. Many ARVN units proved incapable of policing a relatively peaceful region. American troops, partly as a result, had to fight for the same ground again and again.

Accordingly, American casualties rose. By the end of 1967 the United States had suffered 13,000 killed in action and a great many more wounded. In addition, its enemies began to capture some American prisoners, often pilots shot down over North Vietnam. Hanoi took photographs of these prisoners of war (POWs) and paraded them around. The photos frustrated Americans and made them angry, but Washington still assured them that the war was going well.

In late 1967, Lyndon Johnson's government, with Westmoreland in tow, announced a number of optimistic trends. The coming year, 1968, was an election year, and Lyndon Johnson and his party did not want to enter the campaign unless they could claim approaching victory. They hungered for good news. Military leaders, under terrific pressure, gave it to them. (Twenty years earlier, in the exact same circumstances, a French general had stated that he could see "light at the end of the tunnel.") Westmoreland was cautious that autumn of 1967, but he did imply that things were going very well.

Then came Tet.

THE YEAR OF
THE MONKEY

In Asia, many people believe that each year has its own character and that events, good or bad, evolve in a twelve-year cycle. In the ancient Chinese calendar, each year in the cycle is represented by an animal: snake, horse, sheep, monkey, rooster, dog, boar, rat, tiger, rabbit, ox, and dragon. Thus 1968 was the Year of the Monkey. According to ancient tradition each Year of the Monkey should be expected to be filled with energy and turmoil, moments of importance.

So it was to be.

Hundreds of controversies churn through the literature about the war. One of them involves an event called the Tet Offensive. In late January 1968, America's enemies—the VC and, to a much lesser extent, the NVA—came out of hiding and attacked a wide range of targets.

The Vietcong had remained a generally hidden guerrilla group until that point. Why in 1968 did they spring into the open? Did they think the Americans were vulnerable? More likely, did they assume that the Saigon government had lost its hold over the people of South Vietnam?

Some of the planners of the Tet Offensive believed that South Vietnam was ripe for collapse. A simple strong shove might suffice. If the people of South Vietnam could be convinced that Thieu's government lacked the Mandate of Heaven, the people of South Vietnam might well fall into the arms of the Communists. Once that happened, the Americans would have no alternative but to leave.

The American soldiers had come to South Vietnam to "save the South Vietnamese." If the people of South Vietnam asked them to leave, how could the Americans justify staying?

On the other hand, perhaps Westmoreland was correct in late 1967 when he said that the United States was close to victory. If so, was the Tet Offensive a last-ditch, feverish effort by the VC? The evidence remains unclear.

We do know that during the summer of 1967 the leaders of North Vietnam secretly ordered a massive assault in the South, to begin early in 1968, around the Tet holiday. Tet in Southeast Asia is very special. It combines elements of Christmas, Easter, Thanksgiving, and the Fourth of July. Each year, for about a week in February, families get together and celebrate. They set off fireworks, exchange gifts, and eat feasts. Tet is such an important period that, traditionally, enemies put aside their weapons for its duration. Throughout the history of this long war, all participants had usually accepted temporary cease-fires during Tet.

The pattern was about to change.

North Vietnam's plan was complicated. It involved two distinct parts: an NVA assault in the northern section of

South Vietnam, near the DMZ, and a huge Vietcong assault throughout all of South Vietnam.

In I Corps, near the place where the DMZ met the Laotian border, was a small airfield called Khe Sanh. The NVA began to gather near it late in 1967. Westmoreland had intelligence reports about this movement and became convinced that the NVA intended to spring an attack on the Khe Sanh airfield and the marines who protected it, so he ordered his planes to bomb the NVA position. During the next two months they dropped 100,000 tons of bombs on the 5-square-mile (13-square-kilometer) area where American intelligence thought the NVA was massing; this bombardment contained five times as much TNT tonnage as the Hiroshima bomb. The NVA, however, had made sure that they were well dug in. On January 21, 1968, their own artillery opened fire on the Khe Sanh air base. Was this, Westmoreland and Lyndon Johnson wondered, the first stage of another Dien Bien Phu–type assault? In Washington the military built Johnson a scale model of the Khe Sanh base so the president could see, every day, how things were going. He was determined it would not fall as the French base had; he didn't want another Dien Bien Phu, he said.

In fact, the NVA artillery barrage was designed to sidetrack attention from North Vietnam's primary objective. The tactic worked remarkably well. While the president paced the situation room, staring at his scale model of Khe Sanh, the Vietcong moved into place farther south, throughout South Vietnam.

People traditionally travel the roads of Vietnam in the days just before the Tet holiday, moving by cart or foot to their family villages. (In 1968, for example, half of the ARVN troops went home for the holiday.) It would not seem strange, therefore, to see an unusually large amount of traffic during this period. The VC used this situation to get into their positions. Their plan was to spring a simultaneous attack on almost all urban centers in South Vietnam.

The attacks began on January 30, 1968. The assault was incredibly well coordinated. The VC and NVA forces simultaneously hit five of the six largest cities in South Vietnam and thirty-six of the forty-four provincial capitals.

For a moment it appeared that the Communists' gamble was about to succeed. Several town fell to them, including the large city of Hue. In Saigon, Vietcong infiltrators broke through the outer wall and entered the courtyard of the United States embassy, the chief symbol in South Vietnam of American power.

Then the Tet Offensive began to crumble. The offensive had given American firepower the opportunity it had been waiting for. The enemy had actually come out into the open. There he was in plain sight, not hidden in mountainous jungle or in tunnels. Now he could be blasted. And he was. For the next few weeks the Americans fought back, from Khe Sanh in the north—toward which marines drove to relieve their air base—to the towns in the Mekong Delta.

In some places the offensive lasted only a few hours. The infiltrators at the embassy in Saigon never even got inside the embassy door but were stopped in the outer courtyard. In other places the battle lasted longer. Well-armed and tough NVA units held Hue for weeks before they finally succumbed. Khe Sanh was relieved after seventy-seven days.

The fighting was furious—and brutal. American losses were heavy. The Vietcong's were much worse. Over 1,000 Americans lost their lives, but more than 40,000 VC were killed.

In a *military* sense the Tet Offensive was a terrible defeat for the Communists. Not only did they fail to topple Thieu's government, but their losses were so severe that the Vietcong never recovered. Vietcong cadres died in such huge numbers that never again would they be capable of major military ventures.

The United States had won a great *military* victory. They had come to South Vietnam under Eisenhower and Kennedy to bolster Diem's government, eventually to help it fight the Vietcong. American soldiers had concentrated on a single enemy, the VC, "Charlie." The Vietcong had not been eliminated and would continue to be a fierce opponent, but the possibility that they could take over South Vietnam by themselves was removed. In a way America had *won* the war it had come to fight: It had beaten Mr. Charlie. But that goal now turned out to be insufficient. The United States faced another enemy. From the time of the Tet Offensive, America's real war was going to be with the NVA.

During the Tet Offensive the American cause succeeded in other ways. Despite the terrific pressures, Thieu's government did not collapse—nor did the South Vietnamese army, the ARVN, which actually fought well.

Another important result of the Tet Offensive was that it revealed an ugly underside of the Communist cause. At Hue, some local Vietcong committed a major atrocity. They methodically and callously slaughtered thousands of the city's civilians. They simply rounded them up—government officials, Catholic leaders, and intellectuals—and murdered them.

During the early days of the war, Washington officials had justified America's presence in South Vietnam on the grounds that the United States was there, among other things, to prevent a bloodbath. The theory was that if the Communists took over, they might purposely kill huge numbers of people—as, for instance, Stalin had done in the Soviet Union. The intentional bloodbath at Hue was precisely what the American leaders had said

*Marines take cover during the
bitter street fighting in Hue.*

would happen if their enemies won. Here seemed a perfect proof that the war was "justified." The other side had shown themselves to be murderers on a grand scale.

Unfortunately for that argument, not as many Americans were willing to listen any longer. The Tet Offensive had failed badly for the Communists as a *military* act, but in the greater scheme of things it had succeeded.

All wars, it has been wisely said, are political acts— simply a method to achieve political aims. The Communists had long known that fact. The Vietcong, the NVA, and the Ho Chi Minh Trail were all merely cogs in the machinery of a *political* plan to bring Vietnam back together as one country under a Communist regime. The North Vietnamese Politburo, which had supported the Tet Offensive, knew quite well that 1968 was an election year in the United States. They thought that even if Thieu's government was not overthrown, the violence of the offensive might affect the American nation and alter the war. Here they succeeded.

In the United States, opposition to the war had begun quietly. Ever since 1950, most mainstream Americans had tended to accept the necessity of their country's role in the world as an international police. In 1965 that consensus began to change. When the marines first stepped onto the sandy beach near Da Nang, they triggered the early stages of a reaction in the United States.

Only two weeks after the marines landed in Da Nang, the first "teach-in" took place at the University of Michigan. A handful of professors there who did not like the direction of events in Southeast Asia announced that they would lecture to any interested students about how and why the United States had gotten into South Vietnam. The response on campus was surprisingly strong and favorable.

The following month an antiwar rally took place in Washington, D.C. A few weeks later there was a "National Teach-In" at universities all across the nation. In October 1965, protests took place in forty American cities. In a symbolic act of rage a young man named David Miller burned his draft card; during the next several years many other young men would do the same. These early demonstrations reflected a growing antiwar feeling.

Since then, analysts have tried to account for the strong antiwar movement—particularly on the campuses of the nation's most prestigious universities. Why did this particular segment of the population react so strongly against the war?

Some theorists have said that this campus reaction was part of a vast Communist conspiracy to hurt the war effort. It wasn't.

Others have claimed that the demonstrations merely reflected an elitist snobbery by upper-middle-class students. This analysis misses the point. The demonstrators, to be sure, were often self-righteous, congratulating themselves on their own morality and claiming that all their opponents were immoral. But more was involved than simply the attitude problem of some privileged youth. Only a minority of college students actually demonstrated, even at the height of the war.

Some antiwar activists were pacifists by nature—against all wars—"peaceniks," that era called them. Other opponents of the war felt morally troubled by the combination of the obvious brutality of the war and the murkiness of its purpose. Since the goals of the war were never entirely clear, it was hard to swallow the use of napalm and blanket bombing, of "free fire zones" (sections of South Vietnam where every living person was assumed to be an enemy and could be killed on sight), of "harassment and interdiction" sectors (a policy that involved sporadic artillery attacks and occa-

sional bombing of regions through which the enemy might be traveling), of the acceptance of torture—by, among other methods, battery cables attached to the testicles—of prisoners who were only reputed to be enemies. Too many stories and photographs—some in the press, some brought home by returning GIs—portrayed an ugly war, not a crusade.

A case in point involved the Vietnamese village of Cam Ne.

Soon after the marines arrived in Da Nang in 1965, they came under Vietcong attack. They wanted to counterattack. In August 1965 a marine battalion entered Cam Ne, a relatively nearby village with a reputation of housing VC. With them was an American television reporter, Morley Safer, and his CBS crew.

The film of the incident at Cam Ne, which CBS showed on its network news broadcast, portrayed the usual confusion of most battles in Vietnam. Entering the village the marines came under some small-arms fire. Who was shooting at them, and from where, was never clear. At the end of the battle the marines reported that they had killed seven VC. But they had no Vietcong bodies to count. Either none had been killed, or the enemy had carried away their dead and wounded. The only dead Vietnamese on hand was a ten-year-old boy caught in the cross fire. Four marines were wounded.

The most dramatic moment for the television audience came when the cameras showed a marine setting fire to a villager's hut with his Zippo lighter. The official report stated that the marines burned 51 huts, but

Opponents of the Vietnam War
demonstrate in Washington, D.C.

CBS said it was 150. Whichever number one accepts, the image was striking. America had gone to Vietnam to "save" these villagers from Communism. Now Americans were purposely—and under direct *orders*—destroying their homes. It seemed a brutal paradox.

An army major in another action would say, "It became necessary to destroy the town to save it."[11] Some observers began to suspect that this statement represented a horrible metaphor for the whole war.

Another factor in the growing opposition to the war was the attrition policy, which led to a dehumanization of life.

War involves the destruction of human beings. It means maimed and broken bodies, dead children, burned limbs. Soldiers can become almost inured to the gross realities. They did so during the Civil War and the two world wars. But most soldiers in those wars retained a sense of the spark of life. With Vietnam's emphasis on body counts, however, young GIs were asked to *physically count* bodies. Later in the war, they even began to photograph the dead bodies with the new Polaroid cameras that were so readily available in the PXs. If their commanding officers wanted bodies, they would *show* them bodies. The GIs would move the mangled corpses into position for the photographs. A note of black humor often accompanied these grim scenes. Cigarettes were shoved between dead lips. Bodies were placed in grotesque poses.

Stories of such ghoulish activities filtered back home to America, to the place lonely soldiers called simply "the World" (as if they existed in some other place).

American movies and television had always shown plenty of theatrical, storybook deaths, but those were antiseptic—cardboard bad guys falling down when shot. The unreal world of Hollywood and television hardly prepared Americans for the grim reality of Vietnam. Since most Americans had never seen a battle, the filmed scenes of Vietnam—and the emphasis on body counts, on death—were often too intense, too real.

War is always ugly, but civilians, far from the fighting, seldom see it so graphically. Some people after the war blamed the press—the media—for causing the antiwar sentiment to grow. There was a connection, of course, but not because the press slanted the news. It was because the media *showed* at least some of the war.

Morality certainly formed part of the explanation for the antiwar movement, but many cynics have another theory. They have concluded that the real reason for much of the movement—on college campuses especially—was the military draft.

America had maintained a draft system throughout the Cold War. Young males had been liable to be drafted ever since World War II—unless they fell into certain categories. If they were farmers or certain kinds of engineers, they could avoid selective service because their jobs were considered necessary to the nation. If they provided the sole support for another person, they could not be drafted. If they were sickly, insane, retarded, handicapped, or homosexual, they were not supposed to be drafted. Or if they were in school—whether high school or college—they could stay out of the service. As the war heated up and the government increased its draft calls, young males who wanted to avoid it suddenly became "ill" or "insane" or "homosexual." They married and/or had children. They tried a variety of expedients. Some went to Sweden or Canada. A great many simply remained in school.

The number of males at the country's colleges shot up. And they stayed in school—on and on. They worked for graduate degrees in a variety of fields.

In one way the nation benefited, because it suddenly had a large supply of college graduates in necessary occupations. But it seems possible that a certain amount of the antiwar sentiment at the nation's colleges grew out of a sense of guilt, derived from those who were virtually hiding at school, knew it, and didn't like themselves very much. It might have been easier, psychologically, to blame the government.

Another reason for the demonstrations might well have been a growing sense of opposition to any authority figure. The civil rights movement, which peaked in 1964 and 1965, had shown that some authorities—some governors, police, and such—were willing to support laws and systems that were obviously based on bigotry. These revelations damaged the very reputation of authority at the precise moment the war in far-off Vietnam was heating up. The universities that led the way in teach-ins and demonstrations had often been in the forefront of the civil rights movement on campus. And many of the tactics of antiwar demonstrators were adaptations of those used by civil rights demonstrators since the 1950s.

Although the debate still continues over the origin of the antiwar movement, one thing is clear: The movement grew, spreading far beyond the campuses. In October 1967 a rally in Washington drew 50,000, and it included a remarkable number of prominent intellectuals and clergymen.

The addition of the clergy was important. America's clergy forms the backbone of the nation's moral leadership. The fact that many of them had turned against the war gave the movement a semblance of respectability that the often-fevered excitement of the college students had failed to provide.

But it wasn't the anger of student demonstrators or the disillusionment of some intellectuals or members of the clergy that indicated America had turned against the war. In 1965 and 1966, polls had shown that the great mass of Americans did not *support* the war very strongly, but they grudgingly *accepted* it as a necessary task. Later, during the autumn of 1967, polls indicated that opposition to the war had grown to thirty percent of the people. This was an astonishingly large number, but even it had not yet become decisive.

Then, during the period of the Tet Offensive, the feeling of the nation tipped. The images on the television screens, the pictures of death and chaos, were too stark. One famous photograph was both symptomatic and decisive. On February 1, 1968, the chief of the South Vietnamese police was in Saigon. He saw some ARVN troops escorting a Vietcong cadre down the street. The police chief recognized the man as a known killer; he walked up to him, placed his revolver against the cadre's head, and pulled the trigger. Two photographers, witnessing the scene, captured the whole episode on film. The man's pained, terrified face at the moment before he died was seared into America's conscience.

The most important lesson many Americans drew from the Tet Offensive was the stunning fact that it even occurred. Tet had proved that the United States was *not* on the verge of winning the war. Most Americans had accepted the war on the assumption that their army was about to win it, that the other side was getting weaker. But the enemy that took Hue and shelled Khe Sanh was not weak. The shock of Tet made the great mass of Americans turn away from the war. America had spent thousands of lives—and the numbers were growing— and billions of dollars, for what?

Walter Cronkite was the most respected newsman in the United States. He anchored the CBS evening news. He was dignified and strong, with a marvelously warm voice. Americans believed him when he spoke to them of crime or space ventures—or war. In late February 1968, after a trip to Vietnam, he announced to his viewing audience that he no longer believed that the United States could win. Cronkite represented moderate, thoughtful Americans. Polls now clearly showed that the majority of Americans had finally turned against this war.

Nor was this a temporary trend. From this moment on, only a smaller and smaller minority of Americans were inclined to fight to "victory." This great switch of popular sentiment, moreover, occurred in an election year and altered political events.

At the beginning of the year President Johnson could assume that he would be reelected against any opponent. He was not especially concerned when an obscure Democratic senator from Minnesota named Eugene McCarthy announced that he was going to campaign against Johnson. Gene McCarthy even admitted that he knew he had virtually no chance to wrest the Democratic nomination from a sitting president; but he was opposed to the war, and he wanted to offer those Democrats who felt as he did an opportunity to express themselves. It seemed a valiant, but futile, gesture.

After Tet, Gene McCarthy's campaign took off, and Lyndon Johnson appeared more politically vulnerable than anyone had considered possible. In March, Robert Kennedy, the younger brother of John, announced his own candidacy. Two weeks later, Lyndon Johnson, battered in popularity polls, said he would not even accept the Democratic nomination.

In other words, during the two months of the Tet Offensive, Lyndon Johnson had gone from a virtual shoo-in for reelection to a man with only a few months left in office. When Johnson's vice president, Hubert Humphrey, said he would try for the nomination, most Dem-

Lyndon Johnson with members of his National Security Council in 1967. From the left are Secretary of State Dean Rusk, the president, and Secretary of Defense Robert McNamara. In the foreground are Vice President Hubert Humphrey and Secretary of the Treasury Henry Fowler.

ocrats were unimpressed. Lyndon Johnson had become so unpopular, due to the war, that his unpopularity had slopped over onto his vice president.

Hubert Humphrey was in fact a marvelous man, full of energy and optimism. But it was not an optimistic time. During his campaign for the nomination he ran a distant third as McCarthy and Kennedy vied for delegates. They campaigned against each other across the country, essentially ignoring Humphrey. Through April and May they ran neck and neck. Both men came to realize that whoever won the California primary would probably win the nomination—and then go on to defeat Richard Nixon, the certain Republican nominee.

On the night of the California primary, when the votes came in, Robert Kennedy had won. His supporters were euphoric. Kennedy would, it seemed, win the Democratic nomination, beat Nixon in November, and soon afterward as president, end America's involvement in Vietnam. But a few moments after accepting the cheers from his campaigners, Kennedy was killed by an assassin, Sirhan Sirhan.

Two months earlier, Martin Luther King, Jr., had been murdered in Tennessee; riots at the time had swept through black communities across the United States. Now came Kennedy's death. America almost fell apart that summer and the following year. Its internal angers were overflowing. Hubert Humphrey won the Democratic nomination in August, while outside the convention hall in Chicago, police were beating demonstrators.

Political experts were unanimous: Humphrey had no chance. His party was too badly divided. People had come to call Vietnam "Johnson's War." They chanted, "Hey, hey, LBJ, how many kids did you kill today?" Everywhere Humphrey tried to campaign, he was called a murderer, and worse.

But as September became October, the polls indicated a remarkable change. Hubert Humphrey's campaign began to take life. Nixon scrambled to retake the momentum. He said he would get the United States out of Vietnam, that he had a secret plan to do so. He promised "peace with honor."

On election day Richard Nixon won a close contest. The problem of the war was now his to solve.

The goal of any war is to alter the will of your opponent. Everything one does should be based on that single purpose. When North Vietnam had planned the Tet Offensive, it hoped to accomplish several things—and one of them was persuading the United States, during an election year, to get out.

They had accomplished just that.

The lesson was simple and clear. America as a nation was not willing to accept the huge losses that "victory" might have demanded. A minority of the population had wanted to leave the war much earlier. After the Tet Offensive, about an equal number would have fought on, no matter what. The large moderate group between these two—the "silent majority," as Richard Nixon called them—made their minds up in 1968.

The demonstrators had not convinced them; if anything, the increasingly raucous rallies may have made the silent majority hesitate.

Nor was it a knee-jerk emotional reaction, the result of watching ugly pictures of executions and bombings. No, it was a rational, though perhaps unconscious, conviction that the war was *just not worth it*.

Westmoreland had tried a strategy of "attrition"—wearing down the enemy. Ironically, it had worked for the other side. After three increasingly hard years of a tough ground war, it was America that had worn down.

VIETNAMIZATION

From the day Richard Nixon was inaugurated in January 1969, the United States, which had already lost 30,000 men in the war, gradually pulled out of Vietnam, turning the war back over to the ARVN. Lyndon Johnson had actually begun the process late in 1968, but a member of Nixon's government gave it a name, "Vietnamization." The withdrawal, along with peace discussions with North Vietnam, was Nixon's reputed "secret plan," which the press had reported during the 1968 campaign.

Withdrawing from Vietnam was not easy—not if, like Nixon, one wanted "peace with honor," or in other words, not if one wanted to say that the United States had *not* been defeated. You could not simply march your soldiers down to the ships and wave good-bye. So far as the GIs were concerned, 1969 was as bad as or worse than 1968.

Westmoreland had been replaced in June 1968 by General Creighton Abrams, but the war went on about the same. Vietcong snipers still hid in holes or behind trees and shot unlucky or unwary GIs. American soldiers still stepped into punji traps. They still lost their legs and their testicles to "bouncing bettys" (mines that leaped from the ground when triggered, spraying the area with shrapnel). GIs still died in all the awful ways.

In fact, in some bitter ways the war got worse.

One disconcerting fact was becoming evident to the military: the army itself was rapidly eroding. Morale was down, and discipline was collapsing.

The optimistic soldiers of the early years had been mostly well-trained young men who, when they thought about it, accepted the war's necessity. As America's mood soured, as the draft calls increased, as the casualty lists lengthened, the quality of America's "fighting machine" began to decline. The signs were everywhere.

Drugs were plentiful in Vietnam—and cheap. Getting high was easy. One of the grimmest statistics of the war indicates that during these last years one out of every seven soldiers in Vietnam was addicted to heroin, a particularly cruel and demanding drug.

The problem of racism also became especially ugly. The army reflected the anger and divisions back in America, back in "the World." The edginess between the races in the United States led to racial conflicts inside the military, where blacks and whites were squeezed together. There were race riots in military bases in New Jersey, in Germany, in Vietnam.

Crime inside the military also shot up. Petty thievery had always been rather normal, but now the crime statistics indicated far uglier problems. Muggings and murder became all too common. Rape on military facilities became such a problem that female soldiers were warned never to walk alone anywhere on base, especially after dark.

A new word, "fragging," described a terrifying phenomenon. Someone with a gripe against a military superior—usually a sergeant or a lieutenant—would roll a fragment grenade underneath the superior's canvas bunk. The results were often fatal. The culprits were seldom found. The meaning of the word soon expanded to include almost any sort of attack on a military superior. No branch of the service was immune to fragging, but it was worse in the army. Lifetime military people, who had entered the service during a far more disciplined time, were horrified. Every army depends on discipline, on the willingness of individuals to subordinate their own wishes to the will of someone else. When soldiers begin to beat up or kill their officers or their sergeants, can mutiny be far behind? For that matter, can the government depend on its military under such circumstances?

After the war, people would sometimes forget how significantly flawed the military had become by the early 1970s. The generals knew it and privately admitted it to one another. They formed committees to investigate the problems and suggest solutions. It took time, perhaps a decade, but they brought discipline back to the military. The army that the United States sent to the Persian Gulf in 1991 was a far better fighting machine than the one in Vietnam twenty years earlier.

One of the most unpleasant tasks of the military investigating committees was to analyze the matter of American atrocities.

Guerrilla wars, in which it is difficult to differentiate friend from foe, almost always involve atrocities. History is filled with such tales. Ancient Roman armies brutalized North African people in order to subdue them; so did Napoleon's forces in Spain. Vietnam was merely the latest in a long, terrible line.

It is important to remember that the vast majority of Americans fighting in Vietnam did not commit atrocities. Each of them felt terrific stress, fear, frustration, and anger. But most did not intentionally murder innocent civilians. Sadly, some did; but no one should excuse them by suggesting that what they did was "normal." It was not. Yet the deeds of those who did commit atrocities damaged the reputation of their comrades, and it would take years for their nation to recover.

The most famous atrocity occurred in a tiny hamlet called My Lai in March 1968. At the center of the story was a young officer named William Calley.

Calley was a nice, clean-faced young fellow from Florida. In high school he had been a typical, fun-loving boy. He seldom studied hard, but he had average grades. He preferred to ride around in cars, go to movies, and listen to music. He never showed an ounce of viciousness or sadism.

Some time after graduating from high school, Calley learned he was about to be drafted. He quickly volunteered, hoping to enter officer candidate school. A few months later he was in Vietnam. In the process he came to like the military life, and he considered making the army his career. He especially admired his commanding officer, Captain Ernest Medina, a serious, dedicated company commander.

Calley and Medina and their company spent their first weeks in Vietnam getting used to the region. They saw no combat. Then Medina brought his lieutenants and sergeants together one night and told them that they would see action the next morning. They would be taken by helicopters to an area dominated by the Vietcong. They should be prepared for a battle. Calley was in charge of a platoon (somewhat less than forty men). He and his troops would be dropped off in a small hamlet inside the region.

Exactly what Captain Medina then said has since been disputed. Calley later claimed that Medina subtly suggested that his men "take out" the village. Medina later denied that he ordered or even implied such a thing. On the other hand, Calley may well have thought Medina said it.

The next morning in My Lai, Calley's platoon landed and immediately began to search for VC. There were none there. The only villagers to be seen were elderly people, women, and children. (In fact, almost no young men were present at all, almost invariably a sign that a place was a Vietcong haven because VC soldiers would have been elsewhere.)

Some members of Calley's platoon began to beat the villagers. Lieutenant Calley, to his credit, tried to stop them. But the scene, filled with shouts and shrieks, was confusing. Calley started to move the villagers to a nearby drainage ditch. He spoke no Vietnamese, of course, and they spoke no English. He and his men used signals to get the people of My Lai to move. The population was terrified. The women cowered. Some of the children wept. A cameraman, along to photograph a battle, took pictures constantly.

Calley, like most American infantrymen, had an automatic rifle called an M16 that carried twenty bullets in a clip. He and a few others under his direct orders opened fire into the human mass inside the ditch. The Vietnamese tried to run away, but the bullets caught them in the back. Some held their hands up to plead for mercy; others huddled down. Nothing did them any good. Calley remained apparently cool and methodical. He stopped whenever his clip emptied and replaced it with a fresh one.

By that afternoon Calley and several members of his platoon had slaughtered over a hundred people. All of those killed were clearly unarmed civilians. Many of them were small children and babies.

To make matters more shocking, Calley's men (and others in Medina's company) did the same sort of thing *again* the next day.

This was not an isolated act of crazed brutality, done in the heat of battle by men who had seen a great deal of action. This atrocity was committed without provocation. There could be no excuse for it. It cannot be justified—explained, perhaps, but not justified.

It was, however, covered up. It was a year and a half before America learned of the atrocity. Most of the men in Medina's company had left the army by this time and therefore could not be charged for any crimes under United States law. The only people who could be charged were those still in the service, many of them contemplating making the army a career. Calley was one.

The trials of soldiers connected with the incident went on into the early 1970s. Only Calley was finally convicted. He served his sentence in light confinement and was soon released by order of President Nixon.

When stories of the My Lai massacre first surfaced in November 1969, they seemed to confirm what many opponents of the war felt—that the entire war was an atrocious thing, that Americans were *not* the good guys.

The revelations of the massacre arrived just at the moment when the antiwar movement reached its organized peak. The demonstrations during that autumn involved millions of Americans. Small boys wore black arm bands to their fifth-grade classes. Elderly and patriotic grandmothers stood outside their town halls in silent vigils. Half a million individuals from every category of the nation gathered in Washington on November 15, 1969, to express their opposition to the war. The story of the My Lai massacre, appearing in *The New York Times* the very next day, slammed against a nation whose nerves were already raw.

In late 1969, following the revelations about My Lai, sad scenes began to occur at airports throughout the United States. A soldier arriving in the United States, feeling glad to be alive and out of Vietnam, pleased to be back in "the World," suddenly would find himself accosted by a young, self-righteous individual who would *spit* on the soldier's uniform and call him "baby killer." It was a stunning scene, and it happened too many times.

There were other aspects of the war that were almost as shameful or unfortunate as the My Lai massacre. Some soldiers, to show they were "tough," cut ears from their enemies. A few wore these hideous mementos on strings around their necks; others collected them in bottles and took them home as souvenirs. This practice, never as common as casual recollections of the war might indicate, resulted mainly from the body-count policy. When officers insisted on concrete evidence of dead enemies, a few GIs resorted to cutting off ears. The repellent activity spread from there.

A plan called the Phoenix Program, begun under Lyndon Johnson, had focused on the "elimination" (often the assassination) of individual Vietnamese suspected of sympathy for the enemy. After the war, the Communists admitted that Phoenix did have an impact on their activities. But the simple fact of a program of broad-based assassination meant that the United States was pressing outward against the boundaries of "civilized warfare."

And there was Agent Orange. This chemical was mainly used to remove the heavy foliage that enabled the Vietcong to hide in jungle undergrowth or along the waterways of the Mekong Delta. By 1970, America had

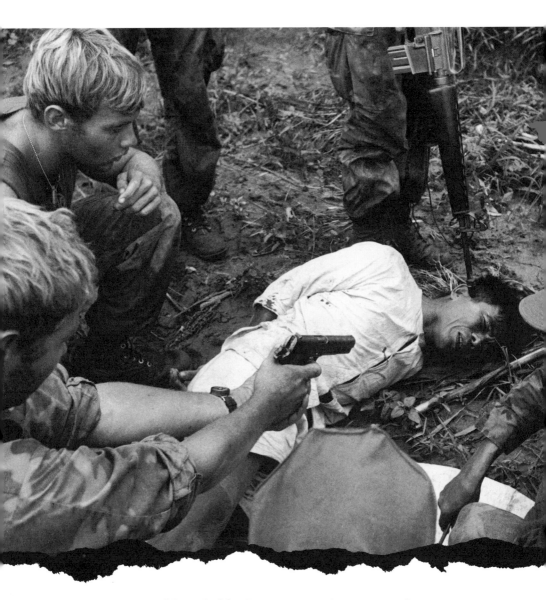

*U.S. soldiers hold a Vietcong captive at gunpoint.
Images of the brutality of war had a powerful influence
on public opinion in the United States.*

sprayed about one seventh of Vietnam's land area with such herbicides. In one military headquarters Americans wryly hung the sign "Only You Can Prevent Forests."

In 1968 a report appeared suggesting that Agent Orange might contain dangerous cancer-causing ingredients. The White House did not actually hear about this report until 1969; then, it almost immediately suspended the chemical's use. But it was probably too late. The herbicide had been dropped from planes and had settled into the soil, where it had entered the water table. Everyone, friend and foe, could have been contaminated—including the Americans. Since 1970, studies have increasingly shown an unusually high rate of some forms of cancer among veterans who were exposed to the chemical.

Richard Nixon, meanwhile, was trying to disentangle his country from the war. He began troop reductions in 1969. He would have liked to have moved faster, but that meant turning the war over to the ARVN more quickly. And despite the death of Ho Chi Minh, from a heart attack in September 1969, the NVA showed no signs of letting up in the fight.

Nixon was determined first to weaken the NVA. To accomplish this end, he concluded that the Ho Chi Minh Trail had to be cut, or "interdicted." Ever since the Tet Offensive, the military had pleaded to be allowed to slice into Cambodia and Laos, to hit the enemy's "sanctuaries." The United States actually had begun bombing the eastern provinces of Laos in 1968 and would continue doing so until 1973. Soon after he took office, Nixon decided to accept the generals' plans for Cambodia. He ordered the bombing of the Ho Chi Minh Trail in that country. This particular bombing had unforeseen political results.

In Cambodia, a canny leader named Norodom Sihanouk had been attempting for years to keep his nation out of the conflict. His government, despite American pressure, had chosen to ignore the North Vietnamese troops and supplies using the Ho Chi Minh Trail in Cambodia's relatively unpopulated eastern provinces. Sihanouk also decided to overlook America's bombing of the trail. He was performing a delicate balancing act.

Then, in March 1970, a coalition of Cambodian politicians ousted Sihanouk. One of them, Lon Nol, became the new head of Cambodia's government. No evidence yet proves that the United States was involved in the coup, but Nixon's government was happy with the change because Lon Nol leaned over backward for the United States.

Immediately after the coup the American military approved an ARVN attack into a section of Cambodia called the Parrot's Beak. This region bulged into South Vietnam only 33 miles (63 kilometers) from Saigon, and American intelligence had long known that it was being used as a staging area for NVA troops about to plunge into South Vietnam.

The ARVN attack into the Parrot's Beak had little effect. But a few weeks later, in April 1970, American ground forces were officially ordered into Cambodia for the first time, into an area called the Fish Hook, about 20 miles (32 kilometers) north of the Parrot's Beak. They were searching, they said, for the command group, COSVN. They did find and destroy some bunkers, and they killed about two thousand people they claimed were enemy soldiers. Soon after, announcing the success of the operation, they left Cambodia.

The Cambodian episode, especially the military "incursion" by American troops, had enormous effects. One result was eventual disaster for Cambodia. The NVA, faced with the bombing and the "incursion," had simply swung farther westward, in effect moving the Ho Chi Minh Trail away from the attacks. The North Vietnamese, now deeper inside Cambodia, backed a small Communist party there that called itself the Khmer Rouge. In April 1975 the Khmer Rouge, led by a vicious killer named Pol Pot, overthrew Lon Nol and captured the government. The Khmer Rouge then began a horrifying process of mass murder.

The incursion also rekindled the fading antiwar movement. Following the huge demonstrations during the autumn of 1969, the movement had lost steam. American forces in Vietnam were obviously being withdrawn, and America's casualties had dropped accordingly. Americans breathed a sigh of relief.

Then came the incursion. Demonstrations erupted everywhere, especially on college campuses. At Kent State University in Ohio, the demonstrations were large and angry. The governor of Ohio, James Rhodes, panicked and called up his state National Guard. At a demonstration on May 4, the young, untrained National Guardsmen opened fire, killing four people and wounding others.

The antiwar movement now had its martyrs. Men wearing *military* uniforms—essentially the same ones worn by the so-called "baby killers" of Vietnam—had shot and killed *unarmed* Americans who were simply protesting the war. This juxtaposition of symbols was too obvious to ignore. A tidal wave of demonstrations flowed across America. In many places, college and high school administrators simply closed their schools, skipping the usual final exams and going right to graduation ceremonies.

No one realized it at the time, but this was the last great, popular antiwar spasm. The movement became

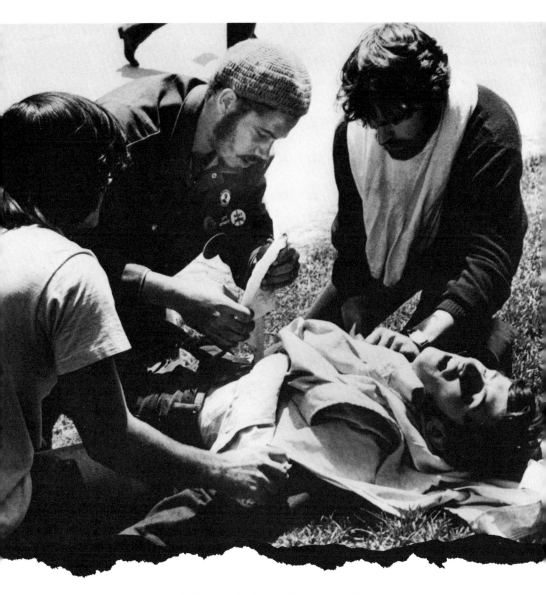

*A victim of the Kent State shootings
receives first aid. The incident, which
left four dead and several others wounded,
sparked a wave of antiwar protests.*

[135]

increasingly irrelevant. In 1971, American combat units in Vietnam fought their last battles and then left. All that remained of America's military presence was its "tail," still in Vietnam primarily to supply the ARVN.

During the fall of 1971, Henry Kissinger, Richard Nixon's chief foreign policy assistant, opened secret peace negotiations in Paris with Le Duc Tho, a North Vietnamese representative. The two men came to several significant agreements before breaking off their talks because they could not resolve their differences over the future of Thieu's government in Saigon. The next year, in September 1972, they met again. This time they hammered out a complete agreement. Thieu, however, refused to accept a section of it that would have allowed NVA troops to control certain parts of South Vietnam (areas, it should be noted, they had been dominating for years). Nixon himself was dubious about this part of the agreement, and he demanded several changes.

Le Duc Tho felt that he was being manipulated and was furious. He decided to demand additional concessions for North Vietnam. It was now Nixon's turn to be angry. He ordered a bombing of several military targets inside Hanoi as punishment for the breakdown of the peace talks. Since this bombing occurred in December, the press immediately dubbed it "the Christmas bombing." The bombing served its purpose: North Vietnam was convinced that Nixon was serious. The peace talks opened again, and this time they took only six days.

The final agreement, ironically, was essentially the same one Nixon and Thieu had rejected only a few weeks earlier; but Nixon was anxious to end America's involvement in Vietnam. To make the agreement more palatable to Thieu, Nixon made two promises. He would significantly increase aid to the ARVN, and he guaranteed, in writing, that if North Vietnam launched a new offensive, he would respond with massive military retaliation. Nixon also noted that he would stop all assistance if Thieu refused to accept the agreement. Thieu grudgingly concurred.

On January 27, 1973, the various representatives signed the Paris Accords. America's war in Vietnam was over. A few hours later Nixon ordered the end of the military draft. Within days, the last American military personnel in Vietnam returned home.

One of the results of the accords was the return of 587 American prisoners of war. Some had been in captivity for years. All had been treated shabbily, some cruelly. They were greeted as heroes, with bands and formal receptions at the White House. They were a symbol that the war was over. GIs who had come home earlier had not, of course, been met with such adulation. But most of them had returned as individuals, not as members of large fighting units, and they had returned long before the war was over.

Meanwhile, events in Washington were about to change the fate of Indochina. Even though the United States was out of Vietnam, American planes continued to bomb the Ho Chi Minh Trail in both Cambodia and Laos. Congressional leaders, concluding that this bombing was both unnecessary and provocative, forced Nixon in August to agree to cease *all* military activities in Indochina. Then, in November 1973, Congress passed, over the president's veto, the War Powers Act. This law required that the president could use American military forces in a particular area only for a limited period of time; the White House would then have to ask Congress for explicit approval to continue.

Another event connected to Indochina's fate was the collapse of Richard Nixon's presidency. His difficulties, in a sense, had started in 1972 with his determination to be reelected in a landslide. He and his staff had cut corners on certain election laws and practices—they had overlooked legal requirements about campaign donations and such. In one incident, a small band of men, connected to the White House, broke into the Democratic headquarters to place secret listening devices and to search for anything that might damage the Democratic party. The Democrats that year maintained their command headquarters in a section of a building complex in Washington called Watergate, which would give its name to the scandal that followed. The Republican burglars were caught by city police. Their arrest eventually led to the arrest of others. During the next year several members of Nixon's staff were taken to court, admitted their guilt for various crimes, and went to jail. Nixon continued to deny any connection to the criminal activities. But eventually someone noted that Nixon had automatic taping devices in the Oval Office; the tapes would prove if he was a liar. They did.

In August 1974, Richard Nixon, to avoid impeachment, resigned from office. His vice president, Gerald Ford, was now president.

The peace pact was a fragile thing. No one really believed the agreement would last very long. It had been designed to offer the United States a fig leaf to cover its nakedness while it withdrew from Vietnam.

Then, in 1975, more than two years after the last American soldiers had departed, North Vietnam attacked the South. Nixon had promised to retaliate if Hanoi tried such a thing, but Gerald Ford had neither the stomach nor congressional approval for a renewal of America's war in Vietnam.

The ARVN collapsed. In April 1975, Saigon stood on the brink of disaster. Washington was deeply con-

A helicopter crewman helps people to the roof of a Saigon building, one of several evacuation points in the city, hours before the North Vietnamese entered the city.

cerned. Thousands of American civilians remained in Saigon and were now in danger of becoming prisoners of the NVA. The United States stationed ships off the coast of South Vietnam and flew helicopters into the capital to begin removing the Americans in the city— along with thousands of Vietnamese who had assisted the American cause and would be in mortal danger if captured by the Communists.

Helicopters arriving in the city landed on the roof of the American embassy and other evacuation points. The embassy had been a symbol of the American presence in Vietnam for years. The fight inside its courtyard during the Tet Offensive had provided television audiences with riveting images. Now, once again, the embassy was the center of attention. Several hundred marines arrived in Saigon to assist in the evacuation and maintain order in the chaotic situation around the embassy building. Photographs of the marines and the military helicopters left an indelible impression on many minds that somehow United States combat forces had been defeated by the NVA, that America was now taking part in a craven retreat. Rather than being seen as it was, as an act of prudence and generosity, the evacuation would become part of the nation's shame.

A few hours after the last helicopter departed, on April 30, 1975, South Vietnam fell at last. Now the Vietnam War was really over.

EPILOGUE

During the next few years Indochina suffered terribly. The nation of Vietnam had finally become a single country, and this was probably for the good. But the Communists began a policy of repression in the South that was cruelly totalitarian. In Cambodia (now officially called Kampuchea), the Khmer Rouge of Pol Pot slaughtered countless people, perhaps millions, in one of the great horrors of modern times. Vietnamese soldiers were ordered into Cambodia in 1978, and a complex civil war churned that land—and Laos—for more than a decade. There was even a brief war between China and Communist Vietnam.

The period of war in Indochina, beginning in 1940 and extending almost unbroken for fifty years, has been a modern tragedy. The losses of human life are incalculable, as is the suffering of millions of people whose lives were disrupted by war.

One of the saddest, and most heroic, residues of those years involved the so-called "boat people." After

1975, hundreds of thousands of Indochinese attempted to escape the nightmare of that land. Many tried a desperate exodus in leaky ships, facing murder and rape by pirates, terrible storms at sea, and starvation. A number of these boat people, however, found their way to communities across the United States. Some of their children became class valedictorians in American high schools.

For half a century the people of Indochina have been participants and pawns in this great tragedy. Was it unavoidable? Were they doomed simply because they were militarily weak, while their land was too valuable—economically and strategically—to remain untouched? Perhaps. If it had not been the French or the Japanese, perhaps some other world power—probably China—would have attempted to control the region.

But how about the United States? Could the United States, at least, have stayed out of it? For that matter, should it have? Or was its presence in Southeast Asia an unavoidable result of the forces of the Cold War? It is hard to know when a war becomes inevitable. It is like looking at the family photographs of a couple, now divorced, and asking when their relationship went sour. Human relations are not easy to explain.

Could the United States have avoided the war in Vietnam? Of course! But when?

How about 1945—when the United States turned its back on Ho Chi Minh?

How about 1950—when Truman decided to support France's war in Indochina?

How about 1954 at Geneva? Or perhaps later: 1961? 1963? 1965?

Each step taken by some American leader—Truman, Eisenhower, Kennedy, Johnson—involved a greater commitment. Under the American political system, it is very difficult for any president to admit serious mistakes. To do so might destroy his reputation. Such an admission would also likely hurt his political party's chances in the next several elections and thereby harm the goals of the president and his party. Nor does a president want to damage the reputation of the United States. Presidents by their very nature are patriots, and they know that one element in America's world stature is its military power. If the United States were to retreat from a military commitment—say, Vietnam—some people, inside the United States and out, would consider this an act of cowardice and weakness.

Thus it was that America was sucked into Vietnam. No president felt he could withdraw. None was willing to say: We made a mistake.

But why did American take its first steps into the quagmire of Indochina? The main reason was the collision between America's policy of containment (of Communism) and one man, Ho Chi Minh. American officials since the time of the Russian Revolution considered nearly all Communists to be subservient to the Kremlin. Since Ho Chi Minh had spent more than twenty years of his life as a functionary of Moscow, it is little wonder that American leaders refused to consider him simply a Vietnamese nationalist and agrarian reformer. Since the Soviet Union was America's enemy, so inevitably seemed Ho Chi Minh.

A terrible thought lingers. If the United States was incorrect in its analysis of Ho, if he was primarily just a nationalist, then the war was "unnecessary."

The United States was not defeated in Vietnam, not in the usual military sense.

During the war Americans never lost a major battle. By 1973, when the last GI left "Nam," the United States was like a large man who has pummeled a smaller opponent. The fight has lasted a long time. The large man keeps knocking the small fellow down, but the little guy is so determined that he keeps rising to his feet. The bigger man's arms have become tired, and his wife is shouting angrily at him to come home. The fight, it seems, might go on forever—and, now that the big man thinks about it, it hardly seems worth it. He can't even remember exactly how it started. So at last he shrugs his shoulders and turns back home. Has he been defeated? No. But he has not won, he has not achieved "victory"—that is, the surrender of his opponent.

In the same way, the United States failed to achieve victory in Vietnam. Moreover, not one of its political goals was gained. Military analysts after the war tried to calculate what went wrong. The most interesting of their conclusions fall into two groups. One states that America's government, especially under Lyndon Johnson, made a mistake by not making sure the nation was completely behind the war.

Johnson occasionally attempted, and so did Nixon, to persuade the American people that the war was justified. Both of them believed, however, that merely saying so would be sufficient. It wasn't. Presidents who lead their nation into a war for unclear reasons have always regretted it if the war has lasted very long.

The second military analysis states that the United States made a mistake in the beginning. It depended on the use of "incremental pressure" (which had worked so well in the Cuban missile crisis). America began small and built up its forces gradually, hoping to press the other side to be "reasonable." But the North Vietnamese had merely increased their forces to match America's military buildup.

By the mid-1980s, America's top brass were determined that, if it ever came to war again, they wanted to enter the war with massive force. The war in the Persian Gulf in 1991 saw this post-Vietnam analysis at work.

Yet one must wonder. Could the United States have "won" the war in Vietnam? Or was the enemy of the United States willing to accept more casualties and a greater cost—of all kinds—than the American nation would have been willing to endure?

Some analysts from the military say that "victory" would merely have required this or that method, generally one they feel wasn't pursued vigorously enough at the time. But none of their "solutions" has ever gotten around the simple willingness of the other side to increase its efforts to match those of the United States. Americans seldom recognized the depth of hatred that the Vietnamese, with their history of struggle against China and France, felt when confronted with the threat of foreign domination.

Moreover, the primary difference between Ho Chi Minh's cause and Diem's and Thieu's was that Ho's was based on the ideals of nationalism and social revolution, while theirs was based on personal loyalty and personal gain. A person motivated by what will best benefit himself must constantly weigh each event to test how it might alter his bank account, his prospects. But a person who fights for a higher goal recognizes that ideals outlive individuals—as Ho Chi Minh's goals outlived him. The war, therefore, was not just a military thing; it was a matter of allegiance.

It would seem as if the war—for America—was like King Canute's tidewaters. The United States, for all its apparent power, could not match a subtle and greater force, the simple will of the enemy to endure, to keep on coming.

[145]

Memories of the war haunt the Vietnam generation. Some veterans still suffer an emotional problem called post-traumatic stress disorder. In the 1980s, when America finally built a memorial to the war's dead, a remarkable monument in Washington that most people simply call the Wall, many veterans laughed bitterly. It seemed too little, too late. But, gradually, some veterans went to see it. And they wept. They lovingly touched the names of buddies who had died in places called Phu Bai and Pleiku, or sometimes a hill with just a number. Middle-aged Vietnam veterans left flowers and medals by the names.

Then others came, and they too wept. In the stark beauty of that Wall there exists some basic truth about lost hopes and dreams, about valor and young men far from home. Some of the last remnants of anger from that era dissolved.

A few veterans have returned to Vietnam to see if they could exorcise their ghosts. An army nurse, Lynda Van Devanter, traveled to Hanoi and was struck by how human the people there seemed. She had hated them so long and so deeply; now she found she couldn't. The people—her ex-enemies—were just like her in so many ways. "War destroys so many things," she wrote about her experiences, "and one of the first to go is the ability to think of the enemy as human beings with a history and a future. . . . You must depersonalize someone to kill him, and that is what the war had done to all of us." [12]

NOTES

1. *Quotations from Chairman Mao Tse-tung* (Peking: Foreign Languages Press, 1966), p. 201.
2. Gareth Porter, ed., *The Definitive Documentation of Human Decisions* (New York: Earl M. Coleman, 1979), I, pp. 64–66.
3. Morley Safer, *Flashbacks* (New York: St. Martin's Press, 1990), p. 22.
4. *Dwight D. Eisenhower, Public Papers, 1954* (Washington: Government Printing Office, 1955), pp. 382–84.
5. John Adams to Hezekiah Niles, February 13, 1818. Quoted in *The Great Quotations*, compiled by George Seldes (New York: Pocket Books, 1967), p. 832.
6. *The New York Times*, January 21, 1961.
7. Porter, II, p. 307.
8. Terrance Maitland et al., *Raising the Stakes* (Boston: Boston Publishing Company, 1982), p. 118.
9. Ibid., p. 130.
10. Arthur Ponsonby, *Falsehood in Wartime* (New York: Dutton, 1928), quoted in Seldes, p. 968.
11. Don Oberdorfer, *Tet!* (New York: Avon, 1971), p. 202.
12. Lynda Van Devanter, *Home Before Morning* (New York: Warner Books, 1983), p. 371.

A CHRONOLOGY

1941   Ho Chi Minh returns to Vietnam and organizes the Vietminh.

       Japan expands its control over all of Vietnam.

       Japanese bomb Pearl Harbor.

1945   World War II ends. Hostility between the United States and the Soviet Union becomes clear.

       Ho Chi Minh declares Vietnamese independence.

       British troops land in southern Vietnam; then return Indochina to France.

1946   War begins between French and Vietminh.

1949   Mao Zedong's Communists win control of China.

       Soviet Union develops atomic bomb.

1950   U.S. President Harry Truman approves support for French war in Indochina.

       Civil war begins in Korea. U.S. enters, then China.

1954 French and Vietminh battle over Dien Bien Phu.

Officials, meeting in Switzerland, agree to Geneva Accords.

France's control over Indochina ends. Ho Chi Minh controls North Vietnam; Ngo Dinh Diem is prime minister of the South.

1957 Cadres of Vietminh begin to organize; they are soon called Vietcong.

1959 North Vietnam begins sending supplies down Ho Chi Minh Trail, which goes through Laos and Cambodia.

1961 U.S. President John Kennedy decides to send more military advisers to assist the Army of the Republic of Vietnam (ARVN).

1963 Diem is overthrown in a coup and murdered.

John Kennedy is assassinated; Lyndon Johnson becomes president.

1964 North Vietnam begins sending regular troops (NVA) down the trail.

General William Westmoreland takes over as head of America's military mission in Saigon.

North Vietnamese patrol boats attack U.S.S. *Maddox,* which is on a radar-spying mission in Tonkin Gulf. This leads to a single U.S. retaliatory air attack on North Vietnam.

Johnson requests and receives congressional support for such actions: Tonkin Gulf Resolution.

1965 U.S. begins sustained bombing of North Vietnam: Rolling Thunder.

U.S. combat troops arrive in city of Da Nang (March 8).

Nguyen Cao Ky becomes premier of South Vietnam. He is the eighth since Diem was ousted.

More troops are sent to Vietnam. Draft is increased in U.S. Antiwar movement begins to organize major demonstrations.

1966   About 5,000 Americans are killed in Vietnam during the year.

1967   Major antiwar demonstrations take place in U.S. (October).

About 9,000 Americans are killed in action (KIA).

Nguyen Van Thieu becomes president of South Vietnam.

1968   NVA forces lay siege to Khe Sanh. The siege lasts over two months.

Tet Offensive begins (January 30). VC, supported by NVA forces, conduct simultaneous attacks on cities throughout South Vietnam. The attacks are crushed; in the process the Vietcong are weakened for good. Communists commit a major atrocity in Hue.

Infantrymen led by William Calley enter My Lai; the most infamous atrocity of America's war takes place (March 16).

U.S. forces in Vietnam reach their peak level of about 540,000.

Johnson announces partial bombing halt, offers to begin peace talks with North Vietnam, and says he will not run again for the presidency (March 31).

Martin Luther King, Jr., is assassinated (April); Robert Kennedy is assassinated (June).

Vietnam peace talks begin in Paris, but negotiations soon break down.

Creighton Abrams replaces William Westmoreland.

Major bombing of Ho Chi Minh Trail in Laos begins.

Richard Nixon is elected president (November); Henry Kissinger will become his national security adviser.

America suffers 14,314 KIA during the year, by far the highest figure of the war.

1969   Nixon begins secret bombing of Cambodia.

Nixon announces he is reducing America's military force (540,000) in South Vietnam by 25,000.

Ho Chi Minh dies (September 3).

Major antiwar demonstrations in cities across the United States.

The story of My Lai is reported in press.

America's KIA equal 9,414 during this year.

1970   Lon Nol overthrows Norodom Sihanouk in Cambodia (March).

American forces move into the Fish Hook in Cambodia to search for Central Office for South Vietnam (COSVN).

National Guardsmen open fire at Kent State University in Ohio, killing four (May). There is major campus rioting across the nation in reaction to both the Cambodian "incursion" and Kent State.

On November 11 (ironically, Veterans Day) no U.S. soldier is killed in Vietnam—the first time in over five years.

KIAs for year number 4,221.

1971   Nixon orders U.S. military in Vietnam to assume only a defensive role.

KIAs equal 1,380.

1972   Nixon goes to China; relations with China begin to improve.

North Vietnam opens a major attack on the South; it involves the heaviest fighting of the war for the ARVN. American air power helps to stem the assault; the NVA, as a result, receive their worst losses of the war.

Kissinger conducts secret peace talks with Le Duc Tho.

Nixon reelected in a landslide.

"Christmas bombing" of Hanoi.

KIAs equal 312.

1973   Paris Accords (January 27). Nixon ends draft; first time since 1949 that the United States has not drafted soldiers.

American POWs released.

Last U.S. troops leave (March 29). Total U.S. losses for the war number over 58,000.

Cease-fire in Laos.

Congress forces Nixon to end bombing of Cambodia (August); this marks the end of America's war in Indochina.

War Powers Act passed over Nixon's veto (November 7).

1974   As a result of Watergate revelations, Nixon resigns presidency and Gerald Ford takes office (August 9).

1975   NVA troops overrun Phuoc Long province (January); when U.S. does not counterattack, Hanoi decides to expand its attack plans.

Major NVA attack; ARVN collapses (March–April).

In Cambodia, Lon Nol flees; the Khmer Rouge take over the country.

Last Americans are evacuated from American embassy in Saigon (April 30). The same day, Saigon falls to NVA.

RECOMMENDED
BOOKS
AND MOVIES

During the war Americans received their information about it piecemeal, in tiny morsels provided by the news media. Most books about it were stodgy or contemplative. The war did not seem to spark great songs or movies or novels, as had some previous wars. After the war was over, publishers and movie-makers hesitated at first to rekindle the era's arguments.

Gradually, beginning in the late 1970s, the nation began to relive the war years. Personal recollections like Philip Caputo's *Rumor of War* (1977) and the film *The Deer Hunter* (1978) found a large audience. In the 1980s the dam burst, and a flood of fictional and nonfictional accounts hit the public. Almost all of this torrent of books and films focused on a single period, the time from about February 1968 (the beginning of the Tet Offensive) to July 1969 (after which the American phase of the war began to fade). To portray the war in Vietnam solely in that period, of course, is to misread it. It would be like trying to understand a vast, complex forest by standing a few inches from its tallest tree and minutely examining its bark. That year was vitally important, and it lends itself to the kind of coherent tales that storytellers prefer. But the Vietnam War was more complicated.

Those interested in browsing through some books on the war in Vietnam and watching a few movies should find the following fruitful.

Books

Baker, Mark, ed. *Nam*. New York: Berkley, 1981.

Caputo, Philip. *A Rumor of War*. New York: Ballantine Books, 1977.

Del Vecchio, John M. *The 13th Valley*. New York: Bantam Books, 1982.

Halberstam, David. *The Best and the Brightest*. New York: Random House, 1964.

Herr, Michael. *Dispatches*. New York: Avon, 1978.

Kovic, Ron. *Born on the Fourth of July*. New York: Pocket Books, 1977.

Mangold, Tom, and John Penycate. *The Tunnels of Cu Chi*. New York: Berkley Books, 1986.

Moore, Robin. *The Green Berets*. New York: Avon, 1965.

Oberdorfer, Don. *Tet!* New York: Doubleday, 1971.

Sack, John, *M*. New York: Avon, 1985.

Sheehan, Neil. *A Bright Shining Lie*. New York: Random House, 1989.

Van Devanter, Lynda. *Home Before Morning*. New York: Warner Books, 1983.

Movies

Apocalypse Now (1979)
Coming Home (1978)
The Deer Hunter (1978)
Full Metal Jacket (1987)
Gardens of Stone (1987)
Good Morning, Vietnam (1987)
Hamburger Hill (1987)
The Killing Fields (1984)
Platoon (1986)

BIBLIOGRAPHY

Bodard, Lucien. *The Quicksand War: Prelude to Vietnam.* Boston: Little, Brown, 1967.

Braestrup, Peter. *Big Story,* 2 vols. Boulder, Colo.: Westview, 1977.

Buttinger, Joseph. *Vietnam: A Dragon Embattled,* 2 vols. New York: Praeger, 1967.

Duiker, William J. *The Communist Road to Power.* Boulder, Colo.: Westview, 1981.

Fall, Bernard. *Vietnam Witness, 1953–1966.* New York: Praeger, 1966.

Gitlin, Todd. *The Sixties.* New York: Bantam, 1987.

Hammer, Ellen J. *A Death in November: America in Vietnam, 1963.* New York: E. P. Dutton, 1987.

Herring, George C. *America's Longest War,* 2d ed. New York: Knopf, 1986.

Hersh, Seymour M. *My Lai 4.* New York: Vintage, 1970.

Karnow, Stanley, *Vietnam.* New York: Viking, 1983.

Lacouture, Jean. *Ho Chi Minh.* New York: Random House, 1968.

Lewy, Guether. *America in Vietnam.* New York: Oxford University Press, 1978.

Michener, James. *Kent State.* New York: Random House, 1971.

Peers, William R. *My Lai Inquiry*. New York: W. W. Norton, 1979.

Pike, Douglas. *Vietcong*. Cambridge, Mass.: MIT Press, 1966.

Schell, Jonathan. *The Real War*. New York: Pantheon, 1988.

Shawcross, William. *Sideshow*. New York: Simon and Schuster, 1979.

Summers, Harry G. *On Strategy*. New York: Dell, 1982.

The Vietnam Experience, 25 vols. Boston: Boston Publishing Company, 1981–86.

Wheeler, John. *Touched with Fire*. New York: Avon, 1984.

Wilson, James C. *Vietnam in Prose and Film*. Jefferson, N.C.: McFarland, 1982.

Zaroulis, Nancy, and Gerald Sullivan. *Who Spoke Up?* New York: Doubleday, 1984.

INDEX

Humphrey, Hubert, 120, *121*, 122-123

Ia Drang Valley, 96
Incremental pressure, 144
Indochina, 17, 46, 141-143
Indonesia, 44
Iron Triangle, 98

Japan, 23-24, 35
Johnson, Lyndon B., 73-76, 83, 86, 100, 105, 108, 120, *121*, 122, 124, 130, 142, 144

Karnow, Stanley, 57
Kennedy, John F., 66-68, 71-73, 82, 85, 110, 142
Kennedy, Robert F., 120, 122
Kent State University, 134, *135*
Khe Sanh, 108, 109, 119
Khmer Rouge, 134, 141
Khrushchev, Nikita, 67, 68, 93
King, Martin Luther, Jr., 122
Kissinger, Henry, 136
Korean War, 31, *32*, 33, 42, 46
Ky, Nguyen Cao, 101

Language, 13, 18
Laos, 17, 44, 46, 77, 82, 99, 132, 137, 141
Le Duc Tho, 136
Lon Nol, 133, 134
Louis Napoleon, 17

MacArthur, Douglas, 100
Maddox, the U.S.S., 74-75
Malaya, 30
Malaysia, 44
Mandarins, 49-51
Mao Zedong, 22-23, 29, 30, 33, 36, 39, 42, 45, 60, 73, 91
Massive retaliation policy, 67
McCarthy, Eugene, 120, 122

McNamara, Robert, *121*
Media, 99-101, 115-117, 119, 131
Medina, Ernest, 127-129
Mekong Delta, 14, 16-18, 94, 109
Mekong River, 14
Miller, David, 113
Missionaries, 16
Montagnards, 11-12
My Lai, 127-129

Napalm, 113
National Security Council (NSC), 31
New Deal, 66
New Frontier, 66
Nhu, Ngo Dinh, *52*, 69, 71
Nixon, Richard M., 66, 122-124, 129, 132, 136-138, 144
North Korea, 31, *32*, 33
North Vietnamese Army (NVA), 75, 85, 86, 91, 93, 95, 96, 104, 106-110, 112, 132-134, 136, 140
NSC-68, 31
Nuclear weapons, 29, 44, 66-67

OPLAN 34A, 74

Paris Accords, 137
Parrot's Beak, 133
Pathet Lao, 82
People's Army of Viet Nam (PAVN) (*see* North Vietnamese Army)
Persian Gulf, 126, 145
Philippines, 30, 31, 44, 87
Phoenix Program, 130
Pol Pot, 134, 141
Post-traumatic stress disorder, 146
Potsdam conference, 25-27